⏚B The Practitioner's Bookshelf

Hands-On Literacy Books for
Classroom Teachers and Administrators

Dorothy S. Strickland
FOUNDING EDITOR, LANGUAGE AND LITERACY SERIES

Celia Genishi and Donna E. Alvermann
LANGUAGE AND LITERACY SERIES EDITORS*

Literacy for Real:
Reading, Thinking, and Learning in the Content Areas
ReLeah Cossett Lent

Teaching Individual Words:
One Size Does Not Fit All
Michael F. Graves

Literacy Essentials for English Language Learners:
Successful Transitions
Maria Uribe and Sally Nathenson-Mejía

Literacy Leadership in Early Childhood:
The Essential Guide
Dorothy S. Strickland and Shannon Riley-Ayers

* For a list of current titles in the Language and Literacy Series, see *www.tcpress.com*

Literacy for Real

READING, THINKING, AND LEARNING IN THE CONTENT AREAS

ReLeah Cossett Lent

Foreword by Jeffrey D. Wilhelm

Teachers College
Columbia University
New York and London

Published by Teachers College Press, 1234 Amsterdam Avenue, New York, NY 10027

Library of Congress Cataloging-in-Publication Data

Lent, ReLeah Cossett.
  Literacy for real : reading, thinking, and learning in the content areas /
    ReLeah Cossett Lent ; foreword by Jeffrey D. Wilhelm.
  p. cm. — (The practitioner's bookshelf)
  Includes bibliographical references and index.
  ISBN 978-0-8077-4943-2 (pbk. : alk. paper)
  1. Content area reading. I. Title.
  LB1050.455.L46   2009
  428.4071—dc22   2008048365

ISBN 978-0-8077-4943-2 (paper)

Printed on acid-free paper
Manufactured in the United States of America

16   15   14   13   12   11   10   09   8   7   6   5   4   3   2   1

Contents

Foreword

WE CAN ALREADY SEE, even this early in the 21st century, that this era is going to place new and untold demands upon us in the domains of literacy, democratic living and citizenry, and disciplinary understanding. Our immediate future will be no place for those who cannot question, inquire, dialogue, use digital discourses, or deeply understand and apply what they know. The great achievement of the book you hold in your hands is that it helps us all proceed powerfully toward all of these ends.

Content-area literacy and learning both get a lot of play in the academic literature and in the wider culture. But most of what I read seems to me to somehow miss the real point, and to miss the power and passion and fun of using literacy to achieve deep understandings, to engage with others and with ideas, and to do real world work. Getting to the point is something Releah Lent knows how to do.

From my perspective as a teacher, I think the situation is urgent. What student of ours is disposable? Which one can we afford to pass on without a powerful sense of literacy's purpose and the facility to pursue problem solving and make meaning with it? I know all teachers would agree that we must reach all our students, imbuing them with a sense of how knowledge and the tools for achieving it truly matter. And yet . . . and yet . . . from a student's perspective the situation is even more urgent. In recent and ongoing studies of the lived-through experience of students in school (e.g., Smith & Wilhelm, 2002, 2004), I have found this daily experience to be of a dire and extremely mind-numbing quality. As one boy asserted to me: "All you do in school is play 'guess what the teacher already knows.'" And another: "Teachers throw you in the pool, wait to see if you drown, then mark it down in their grade book."

Young people want to be engaged in significant work; they want to work through and in relationship with peers and teachers; they want to be assisted to know, do, be, and become more than they currently are; they want to move toward competence and expertise. Both research and classroom experience tell us that there is relatively little instruction that promotes this kind of engagement and deep learning (see, for example, reviews in Smith & Wilhelm, 2002; Wilhelm, 2007). Releah Lent's current book offers an antidote to this situation.

I am currently working with a group of 10 students and 10 master teachers on a project for both inducting student teachers into the profession and re-energizing experienced teachers. Our work is invigorating and exhausting, uplifting and challenging. Together we are engaged in joint teacher research projects to promote reflective teaching. This project has reinforced to me yet again the complexity of teaching, the difficulty of knowing and motivating one's students, the ever-evolving hydra-esque nature of literacy, and the work that it can do personally, in the disciplines, and in the world. As I read this book on content-area literacy, I found myself appreciating every page and applying what I was learning to this current project, as well as to my own teaching with both middle-schoolers and with university students.

To get to my own point: This is an immensely hopeful and forward-looking book with immediate applications. It provides a very useful and reassuring toolbox in a time of challenge and change, of problems and possibilities.

This book is at once theoretical, thought-provoking, and practical. It is clear-eyed and realistic about the obstacles facing teachers and students, and at the same time refreshing and positive in its coherent approach to addressing the tasks that are set before us. Releah Lent recognizes the challenges from the history, traditions, structures, and policies that surround schools, as well as the demands placed on democratic citizens by the 21st century—and she knows how to implement approaches and use various techniques that can work within current structures and help to overcome typical shortcomings. As her book unfolds, she makes many explicit and implicit arguments about the future of literacy and the possibilities for re-energizing teaching and learning that gets at what I would call "the heart of the matter" about using literacy to achieve usable understandings. (And, as I remind my student teachers, if we are not teaching for usable understandings, then what in the heck are we teaching for?) It does this against the backdrop and big picture of 21st-century literacy as a meaning-making, problem-solving pursuit necessary to disciplinary thinking and understanding. Embedded in the arguments are a wealth of ideas about how to promote teaching for understanding.

This book compellingly takes up the question: What is the problem to which engagement, strategies, digital and disciplinary literacies, and much more are the answer? It helps the reader to see the contexts in which expertise in literacy is situated, co-produced, and honed to become meaningful and useful. It is a book that is respectful of disciplinary work, of teachers, and most of all and most importantly, of students and their various and immediate needs, including that most important one of being assisted to do meaningful work so that they may soon do that work on their own.

—Jeffrey D. Wilhelm,
Boise State University, 10/06/08

Acknowledgments

IT IS THROUGH TEACHERS AND STUDENTS that books such as this come to life. I want to thank Holmes District for the opportunity to work with their schools and to come to know their educational community, particularly their exemplary reading coaches. I especially thank Ingrid Gillman, who opened her classroom to me and provided wonderful photographs of her students engaged in active literacy.

I am also indebted to Pat Suggs, whose enduring commitment to adolescent literacy led to our collaboration on a progressive literacy initiative for secondary content-area teachers. The project became the foundation for this book. Many other excellent teachers, such as Katherine Meraz and Joan Albury, shared with me their ideas for interactive practices, and I, as well as their students, am thankful that they are in the classroom.

I am deeply appreciative of my editor, Meg Lemke, for her encouragement and remarkable editing talents as we fashioned this book into one that is truly a practitioner's guide. I am also grateful for the series editors' guidance in the early stages of the proposal.

As always, I could not have finished this book without my insightful and patient husband, Bert, who is turning into a first-rate editor. My gratitude and love go to him and to my dear friend Gloria Pipkin, a real-life editor, for their support, wisdom, and willingness to read my work as many times as it takes.

Introduction

I RECENTLY FOUND A BOOK in an antique shop titled *The Improvement of Reading* by Linda Cole, copyright 1909. I read the first paragraph several times and then decided that I had to have the book as a reminder of how the struggle for the right to literacy is universal and timeless. The author began the book in this way:

> Ability to read not only marks the difference between the literate and the illiterate person; it is also an absolutely necessary basis for other subjects in curriculum. To be sure, in the earliest grades a child may compensate for a deficiency in reading by accurate listening and a good verbal memory, but the time soon comes when progress in all academic subjects very nearly ceases unless he can read. It is therefore essential that teachers should understand the nature of the reading process, in order that they may give the greatest possible aid to pupils in the mastery of his fundamental educational tool—the ability to read.

With the exception of recognizing that females also need to learn to read, little has changed in nearly a century. Reading is still a fundamental educational tool, although in the 21st century, what we read has changed much more than our reasons for reading. We still want students to read for information, of course, but also to make connections, to explore worlds vicariously that cannot be accessed physically, to experiment with emotions without having to face their repercussions, to appreciate a well-turned phrase or an apt metaphor. We want students to read to discover their place in humanity and to understand themselves through the actions of characters whose faces mirror their own as well as through characters they would never hope to emulate. We want them to read critically to discern truth from spin, to analyze, shape, challenge, or confirm their deepest beliefs. We want them to read in order to know.

READING THE FUTURE

Unfortunately, in classrooms all across the country many teachers are convinced that students either can't or won't read. They may cite the litany of excuses given by their students as proof that the era of reading has passed. Do any of these sound familiar?

> "I don't have time to read. I have (a job, extracurricular activities, family chores . . .)"
> "I tried to read it, but it is just too boring."
> "Yeah, I read it; well, I skimmed it anyway."
> "I fell asleep reading."
> "The author uses too many words I don't know. I just don't get it."
> "I can't keep my mind on the topic no matter how hard I try to concentrate."

We often forget that students read every day: text messages, blogs, driver's license manuals, videogame guides, Internet sites, magazine articles, notes from friends, graphic novels, young adult literature, song lyrics. Most secondary students *can* read, but they may have difficulty reading the texts we are assigning. Our challenge is to engage students in such a way that they transfer and hone the skills they already use for out-of-school reading to access knowledge in the classroom. If we want students to think critically about and engage actively with the concepts inherent in content-area study, then they must both be able to master the mechanics of reading and *comprehend* what they are reading. Students who have gleaned only enough information to pass a standardized test will not deeply understand the content, nor will they be sufficiently prepared for the demands of today's increasingly complex world. Peter Sacks is definitive in his compelling book *Standardized Minds*:

> Evidence strongly suggests that standardized testing flies in the face of recent advances in our understanding of how people learn to think and reason. Repeatedly in the research over the past few years, especially in the grade school area (K-12), one finds evidence that traditional tests reinforce passive, rote learning of facts and formulas, quite contrary to the active, critical thinking skills many educators now believe schools are encouraging. (Sacks, 2001, p. 9)

Indeed, the warnings are dire: Many students are graduating without the critical skills necessary for future success. The Alliance for Excellent Education, in an issue brief on teaching for the 21st century, found that "most students will need at least some post-secondary education to earn a decent wage." They concluded that high schools are failing students by not preparing them for college, noting that teachers must "teach rigorous content so that students can apply knowledge in new situations, and use teaching methods that engage students in learning to reason, write, and use information in complex ways" (2007, p. 1).

The Partnership for 21st Century Skills contends that one of the challenges facing schools is that knowledge is much broader today than what was required of graduates even a few years ago. Such knowledge includes global awareness, civic literacy, communication skills, critical thinking, problem-solving skills, leadership, ethics, and social responsibility, to name a few. Although we may agree that the core subjects also outlined by the Partnership—English, reading, mathematics, science, foreign languages, civics, government, economics, the arts, history, and geography—are essential for a well-rounded education, the question still remains: How are students to develop skills in these subjects if they are unable or unwilling to expand their knowledge through content-area reading?

As the Alliance for Excellent Education noted in its report titled *Literacy Instruction in the Content Areas: Getting to the Core of Middle and High School Improvement,*

Inasmuch as the academic content areas comprise the heart of the secondary school curriculum, content area literacy instruction must be a cornerstone of any movement to build the high-quality secondary schools that young people deserve and on which the nation's social and economic health will depend. (Heller & Greenleaf, 2007, p. 1)

Students must learn to read in ways that empower them as thoughtful consumers of subject-area content.

How are teachers to assist students in becoming proficient, critical readers while still maintaining a focus on their subjects? Is it realistic to expect a teacher to teach calculus or the scientific method and, at the same time, foster literacy skills? This book examines ways to incorporate practices into the curriculum that infuse the components of reading into content-area curriculum but do not supplant it. Reading, like listening and speaking, should permeate any curriculum as a tool for learning, but generic reading strategies are not the "multipurpose" tool we once believed them to be. Throughout this book, I ask teachers to consider reading as it relates to their specific content area. How does reading in math, for example, differ from reading in science?

INFUSING READING INTO CONTENT-AREA STUDY

This book will serve as a guide for teachers, reading coaches, and administrators as they help students become independent readers of all texts: print-based, digital, and visual. I present these concepts not as definitive answers, but as springboards for reflection about how reading can become a conduit for relevant, meaningful, content-area learning. In the spirit of such inquiry, each chapter offers the theoretical underpinnings for various components of reading and practice examples for literacy instruction, as well as varied resources for continued study.

Chapter 1, "Engagement: Reading's Missing Link," examines the vital role of engagement and motivation, aspects that are often missing from secondary classroom instruction, and offers learning frameworks that can be applied to all subjects. This chapter also discusses the importance of active reading and provides practices to facilitate the active reading process.

Chapter 2, "Building Background for Reading," offers activities for building and activating students' background knowledge since studies find this practice to be one of the most important for developing deep understanding.

"Making Meaning through Reading," Chapter 3, focuses on content-area texts and argues that students must learn to read proficiently in different disciplines as experts in those disciplines read. Scientists, for instance, utilize specific skills or strategies when reading, such as determining what is important in data, synthesizing various pieces of information to find a pattern, and recognizing specialized vocabulary. As an example, physicists understand the term *wormholes* in a journal article to mean something entirely different from the way an arborist may use the term to refer to tree damage by insect larva. This chapter also emphasizes collaborative study through dialogue and generating questions.

Chapter 4, "Vocabulary: The Key to Meaning," challenges teachers to differentiate vocabulary instruction and provides essential tools to support the practice. Readers can also access a variety of "before, during, and after" reading activities to provide rich and conceptual vocabulary study that goes well beyond the common, but ineffective, practice of assigning lists of words with definitions.

"Reading for Deep Understanding," the topic for Chapter 5, explains how to help students read strategically while monitoring their comprehension, especially when they encounter difficult or unfamiliar text. This chapter argues that providing students with challenging reading across the curriculum will increase their content-area knowledge, self-efficacy, and motivation, components necessary for intrinsic learning.

Chapter 6 looks at the timely topic of critical reading, and provides ways to help students read as healthy skeptics in examining various print and other media texts for bias and accuracy. It also addresses the concept of critical literacy, the notion that texts have multiple meanings with multiple perspectives based on an author's intent and motives.

Chapter 7 focuses specifically on online reading and the unique comprehension challenges in this complex medium. The chapter offers an examination of the skills needed to access online reading, many of which are similar to those for reading nondigital texts. Since online reading is by nature interactive, the chapter includes comprehensive instructions and blank forms for engaging students in a collaborative, online reading inquiry project.

The final chapter, "Expanding Meaning," summarizes the book's message of integrated literacy and suggests resources for infusing the curriculum with a variety of content-rich texts. Such materials help students expand their reading and vocabulary skills as they integrate out-of-school literacies with the academic reading necessary to carry them confidently into the future.

MOVING FORWARD WITH HOPE

There is no doubt that the current responsibilities of teachers are daunting. Educators are expected to help students become thoughtful readers, critical thinkers, and autonomous learners while managing to teach an ever-expanding curriculum and deal with high-stakes testing and the hormonal swings of multitasking teenagers. Such demands require that students take on more of the responsibility for their learning as adept and independent readers. Yet, as students move toward independence, they must realize that the best resource they have is still you, their teacher, to coach them through the process of reading in the discipline that you know best.

The *Reading Next* report ended on an urgent note, one that has increased in urgency each year since the report's publication in 2004: "We all hold a stake in the literacy achievement of youth, and if we do not rise to meet this challenge today, we risk our cadre of struggling readers and writers facing a future of sharply diminishing opportunities" (Biancarosa & Snow, 2004, p. 31). Despite this caution, there is an abundance of hope. With the appropriate use of content-specific strategies, a clear understanding of the role of reading in academic subjects, and engaging instructional practices, teachers can show students how reading can be used as a "fundamental education tool," as Linda Cole reminds us in her 1909 book—one that will enable students to unlock meaning within the classroom, extend learning outside of school, and access knowledge for life.

CHAPTER I

Engagement: Reading's Missing Link

IF WE COULD SEE THROUGH THE WALLS of many second-ary classrooms across the country, we might witness a scene that looks something like this: Thirty or so students in an English or social studies class are sitting at desks or, in a more progressive classroom, arranged around tables. Some are talking quietly, others have their heads resting on their books, and a few are staring off into space as if viewing an invisible movie that is only moderately interesting. Their teacher, an enthusiastic young woman with a freshly minted degree, tells the class that they will find the next unit *fascinating*, especially since it includes the diary of Anne Frank, "One of the most remarkable first-person accounts to come out of

World War II. You may have heard about Anne Frank, but you will feel like you are there with her in that tiny attic as you read her diary. After that," she continues, "we will study another type of memoir written by a boy who survived the Holocaust, *Night*. This book had a profound effect on me when I was your age. I promise that you will never view life the same way after spending the next few weeks with Anne Frank and Elie Wiesel." The response to such a motivating introduction is silence. The teacher sighs and, with admirable determination, begins passing out copies of well-worn paperbacks. Unfortunately, this scenario is more the rule than the exception.

"Today more than two thirds of all eighth and twelfth graders read at less than a proficient level" (Heller & Greenleaf, 2007, p. 2). Teachers bemoan the fact that so many of their students, even those classified as proficient readers, resist reading assigned texts in the classroom or completing reading assignments at home. Research supports this anecdotal evidence with statistics that show intrinsic motivation for reading decreasing in middle and high school (Guthrie & Anderson, 1999). While comprehension and vocabulary strategies abound in textbooks, commercially packaged programs, and online, they often lack the key component of reading: engagement.

ENGAGEMENT IN READING

Guthrie and Anderson (1999) define reading engagement as the "joint functioning of motivation, conceptual knowledge, strategies, and social interactions during literacy activities" (p. 20). A report from the Florida Center for Reading Research outlines three "big ideas" to improve literacy for adolescents, and one of these specifically addresses engagement. "We must take the problem of motivation and engagement in content area classes and all reading classes very seriously. We must engage student motivation more broadly if literacy levels are going to increase significantly" (Torgesen, 2007, slide 16). How important is engagement? Multiple studies have found that engagement is strongly related to reading achievement (Guthrie, 2001). Motivated students give more thought to their reading and use strategies more effectively (Guthrie & Anderson, 1999). Assigning reading or using comprehension and vocabulary strategies without paying attention to student engagement is putting the proverbial cart before the horse, an arrangement that will not take us where we wish to go.

Compare the following picture of engaged readers to the students described at the beginning of the chapter. It is an election year and students in an American government class read newspaper articles about the local candidates for state representative. They then write questions based upon what they learned about the candidates from their reading and invite the candidates to participate in a student-facilitated forum where a panel asks questions submitted by their classmates. Afterward, students create flyers with bulleted quotes from each of the candidates to distribute at the polling booths on election day. These students, with the help of a knowledgeable teacher, imitate researchers' description of engagement: ". . . motivated to read for a variety of personal goals . . . strategic in using multiple approaches to comprehend . . . use knowledge actively to construct new understanding from text . . . interact socially in their approach to literacy." They are engaged readers, "decision makers whose affects [expressions] as well as their language and cognition play a role in their reading practices" (Guthrie, 2001, p. 2). The promise of engagement offers optimism not only for teachers of striving readers but for all of us who are concerned about students' disinterest in school, a factor that increasingly manifests itself in a plummeting graduation rate.

ENGAGEMENT IN LEARNING

Although many researchers have examined the issue of engagement, Brian Cambourne, head of the Centre for Studies in Literacy at Wollongong University in Australia, has studied this topic for over 30 years. His model for engagement is one that can be easily infused into all content-area classes (Cambourne, 1995). Engagement, according to Cambourne, is the bullseye of learning, with other conditions facilitating students' aim. In Cambourne's later work (2008), he describes his model as "learning how to mean" and notes that engagement is only possible if learners can make sense of what is being demonstrated. With such a model, students do not decode text in search of isolated bits of information or for the purpose of passing a test, but instead use the process of reading to make sense of the events, facts, and opinions that infuse the text.

Cambourne's Conditions for Learning

The conditions of learning outlined in Figure 1.1 take place simultaneously, rather than in a linear fashion, much as learning itself occurs.

Cambourne contends that engagement often involves risk-taking, a behavior students have mastered outside of class, but in many classrooms intellectual risk-taking is quashed under the thumb of high-stakes testing. Additionally, our system of education

FIGURE 1.1. Cambourne's Conditions of Learning

Condition of Learning	General Application
Immersion	Learners will be immersed in the topic of study. The curriculum might include extended opportunities for engagement with a wide range of texts as well as writing, speaking, listening, viewing, and participating in activities related to the content.
Demonstration	Learners will have many demonstrations before attempting new learning. These demonstrations may take various forms, such as observing, hearing, and experiencing.
Expectation	Learners and teachers must hold expectations that students can and will succeed. This fosters students' self-efficacy, their ability to feel competent in dealing with learning tasks and thus willing to work harder to achieve success. According to Cambourne, expectations from those to whom the learner has bonded are most powerful.
Responsibility	Learners will acquire and maintain responsibility for learning tasks by being allowed to make decisions about such factors as what, when, and how they will learn.
Employment	Learners will be afforded time and opportunities to "employ" or use new learning in relevant and meaningful ways.
Approximation	Learners will "approximate" learning, which means they will feel safe to take risks and make mistakes. Students will understand that mistakes are an essential part of learning.
Response	Learners must have appropriate, timely, relevant, nonthreatening feedback from teachers and knowledgeable others.

often defines *achievement* in ways that minimize engagement. For example, if students pass a test on the skeletal system, the poetry of Dylan Thomas, or quadratic equations, we feel reassured that they have had a successful learning experience. This success is translated into grades that mark the student's level of achievement. How would Cambourne's Conditions for Learning look in the social studies or English class described earlier, where the teacher is asking students to read texts such as *Anne Frank: The Diary of a Young Girl* (Frank, 1993) and *Night* (Wiesel, 2006)? Figure 1.2 provides an example of resources and activities that would facilitate engagement and deep learning about the Holocaust. Note that Chapter 6 provides detailed information about how to use text sets and Chapter 2 offers information on picture books for older students.

Other Models of Engagement in Learning

Other models of engagement include components that are similar to Cambourne's Conditions of Learning, including the following by Guthrie and Wigfield (2000). In their study on engagement and motivation cited in a paper commissioned by the National Reading Conference, titled "Effective Literacy Instruction for Adolescents," they found that instruction calls for

- Student motivation (including self-efficacy and goal-setting)
- Strategy use (e.g., using prior knowledge, self-monitoring for breaks in comprehension, and analyzing new vocabulary)
- Conceptual knowledge (e.g., reading trade books to supplement textbook information, viewing videos, and hands-on experiences)
- Social interaction (e.g., collaborating with peers on a science project and discussing an Internet search with the teacher). (p. 7)

Think about a topic that you teach regularly, perhaps one that you or students don't find particularly engaging. Good candidates may include Jonathan Edwards's "Sinners in the Hands of an Angry God" (1741) in English, the inner workings of the electoral college in social studies, or the laws of sines and cosines in math. Work with your department or a colleague who teaches the same

FIGURE 1.2. Cambourne's Conditions of Learning Applied to the Study of the Holocaust in Social Studies/English, Grades 8–12

Primary Resources: *Anne Frank: The Diary of a Young Girl*; *Night*

Condition of Learning	Description
Immersion	Immerse students in the study of the Holocaust through videos such as Spielberg's "Survivors of the Holocaust," online research through the United States Holocaust Memorial Museum (www.ushmm.org), and primary documents, maps, and historical data. Teachers may collaborate to create text sets of short stories, fiction, nonfiction, and poetry related to World War II. Have students create visual displays on walls or bulletin boards. Guest speakers may also be invited to the class.
Demonstration	Show students how "expert" readers gain meaning from texts by making your thinking visible as you read aloud, often called "thinking aloud." Suitable texts include picture books such as *The Yellow Star of Denmark* (Deedy, 2000) or *Fireflies in the Dark: The Story of Friedl Dicker-Brandeis and the Children of Terezin* (Rubin, 2000) and young adult novels such as *Number the Stars* (Lowry, 1990) or, for older readers, *The Boy in the Striped Pajamas* (Boyne, 2006). Use nonfiction as well, such as *Anne Frank: Beyond the Diary: A Photographic Remembrance* (Verhoeven, Van der Rol, Quindlen, & Langham, 1995) or, for high school students, *The Sunflower: On the Possibilities and Limits of Forgiveness* (Wisenthal, 1998). Graphic novels such as *Mendel's Daughter: A Memoir* (Lemelman, 2007) or *Maus* (Spiegelman, 1986) provide texts in a different genre.
Expectation	Survey students before beginning study to determine students' prior knowledge and attitudes about the Holocaust. They may write about their experiences or background knowledge as a way of forming realistic and personal expectations.
Responsibility	Students will gain responsibility when given choice in reading and learning tasks. For example, allow students to decide which of the two books, *Night* or *The Diary of Anne Frank*, they want to read, and allow them to choose tasks and texts used for collaborative study.
Approximation	Encourage students to try out their new learning in a safe environment, often with partners or in small groups. Resist the urge to give tests or "correct assignments" while learning is ongoing. Instead, monitor students' progress through exit slips, learning logs, and participation in discussions.

Condition of Learning	Description
Employment	Provide opportunities for students to use new knowledge through research projects, presentations, or online communication. Older students may research the nature of genocide, for example, by reading about genocides such as Darfur's tragedy in *The Translator* (Hari, 2008).
Response	Provide feedback that fosters learning beyond graded assessments. *Show* students how to revise their work and comprehend difficult text. Ongoing dialogue (a form of response) will provide a meaningful structure for in-depth learning.

subject to create a plan for making the topic more engaging by using either of the models of engagement described in this section of the chapter.

ACTIVE VERSUS PASSIVE READING

Domain-specific reading—that is, reading that relates to specific subject areas—involves much more than passively reading words on a page or using textbooks to answer worksheet questions. Perhaps the best contrast to engaged reading is what many teachers call "fake reading," a rather persuasive behavior that students use to convince teachers that they are really reading. Although students' eyes may move appropriately, their minds do not "see" the words in the text. Reading for meaning involves students' active participation with texts as they ask questions, form opinions, make inferences, find connections, and generally feel confident enough to evaluate what they are reading in terms of credibility, interest, and importance. Figure 1.3 compares the behaviors of active and passive readers.

Practices for Active Reading

How can teachers help their students become active readers instead of allowing the text to pass them by? The following activities can be incorporated into any academic content area to encourage engaged, dynamic reading and learning.

Figure 1.3. Behaviors of Passive and Active Readers

Passive Readers	Active Readers
accept a purpose that is imposed from someone else (e.g., to pass a test, to find an answer, to complete an assignment).	create a purpose that often has intrinsic value (e.g., to satisfy curiosity, apply new learning, share knowledge with others, use information for a relevant task).
rarely ask questions or disagree with what they are reading. They are, in effect, "invisible" participants, perhaps because they have come to believe the author is omniscient and holds all the power.	question the author (e.g., why did the author make this point, use this analogy, create this character). Readers may even disagree with the author, mentally arguing the correctness of their positions.
may decode words proficiently but take meanings literally and are unable to "read between the lines."	make inferences and understand nuances that are not immediately evident. They "get" metaphors, analogies, and extended examples.
rarely compare what they are reading to other texts, their own experiences, or the world at large.	filter the text through their own lens, using their background knowledge to expand understanding.
don't believe they are capable of reading deeply and often rely on others to gain sufficient information to pass the class or satisfy those in charge.	believe they can make meaning and are willing to work toward making that happen.
may not be aware of when meaning breaks down and do not have strategies to repair comprehension.	monitor their comprehension, recognize when meaning breaks down, and employ strategies to regain understanding.
find most reading "boring."	generally like to read, often becoming passionate when reading texts about topics that interest them.
do not understand that they should adapt how they read according to what they are reading. They often become frustrated when they encounter text structures with which they are not familiar.	realize that text changes according to its content, purpose, and audience, and they vary their reading to accommodate such changes in text.

Show students how to interact with the text by using sticky notes or two-column note-taking forms to record their thoughts, responses, and important points. When using two-column notes, students should write the page number in the left column and responses in the right column. Following are prompts that students can use until the interaction becomes internalized.

- Write one statement that interests you and one statement with which you disagree.
- Write three questions about what you have read so far.
- Write something from your own experience or the news that helps you make a connection to what you are reading.
- Write one idea from the text that you would like to discuss with another student.
- Write about something that confuses you.

Practices for Collaborative Reading

Engaged readers interact socially. "When students in a small-group activity believe that they can trust other students to listen and accept their suggestions, they become personally invested in the group activity" (Guthrie & Anderson, 1999, p. 35). Joan Albury, a high school math teacher, allows students to collaborate often in her classes. For example, she explains how students enhance understanding of linear equations through interaction: "I show students three ways to write a linear equation: Slope-intercept form; point-slope form; standard form. I tell them to pick their favorite form and defend it or convince someone else that it is the best one." She uses another group activity to help students with the difficult concept of order of operations: "I have small groups create a problem by letting one student write a number. The second student adds a mathematical symbol such as +, -, ×, or ÷ and then another number. The paper continues being passed until there are sufficient steps to work the problem. The group then uses the order of operations to work the problem."

At every opportunity, involve students in dialogue before, during, and after reading. Students may, for example, stop reading at the end of a certain page (or at the end of a scene in a video) and discuss specific points, such as "Why does ___ happen?" "What would you do if . . . ?" "What do you think will happen next?"

"What is the point?" Chapters 3–6 contain suggestions for collaborative activities, and Chapter 7 describes an online group research project that could be adapted for other content-area uses.

ENGAGEMENT AND MULTIPLE INTELLIGENCES

I met an enthusiastic science teacher at a conference recently named Katherine Meraz who described an interactive science notebook she developed to help her students become more actively engaged in biology. The example she showed me was colorful and large, reminding me of an advanced type of pop-up book, the kind my own children found so intriguing. Katherine understands that many of her students do not possess strong verbal and mathematical intelligence, attributes traditionally valued in schools, so the notebook helps students with varying "intelligences" become more successful. She asks students to personalize the front and back covers of their notebooks with pictures, words, and other symbols related both to biology and their own lives. Inside, there are a variety of interactive tools, such as a template of an appointment clock, where classmates' names are written to designate a scheduled time for collaborative study. See Figure 1.4 for a visual of this activity.

FIGURE 1.4. Appointment Clock in Interactive Biology Notebook

The notebook itself is "stuffed" with other tools, such as construction paper stapled onto pages where students define and illustrate new vocabulary. There are sections for student questions, pages without lines to encourage drawings (such as the life cycle of a cell), and even a page for homework stamps to indicate when students complete outside assignments. This notebook provides for differentiated instruction as well as a means for Katherine to conduct formative assessment. More importantly, it allows students to participate in learning in a variety of engaging ways.

Howard Gardner, creator of the theory of multiple intelligences, provides educators such as Katherine with a framework for engaging students in both learning and literacy based on a broadened view of intelligence. Gardner's definition of intelligence addresses the capacity to "solve problems or fashion products" (Gardner & Hatch, 1989), supporting current research about the importance of creative and critical thinking. Gardner also seemed to predict the role of a 21st-century teacher when he wrote,

> An effective teacher functions as a "student curriculum broker," ever vigilant for educational prosthetics—texts, films, software—that can help convey the relevant contents, in as engaging and effective a way as possible, to students who exhibit a characteristic learning mode. (1991, p. 246)

Understanding Multiple Intelligences

What are these characteristic learning modes? They are learning strengths, or what Gardner terms "intelligences," that differ from student to student. By identifying predominant intelligences, a student may come to understand why he may be a star on the soccer field (bodily-kinesthetic intelligence) but have difficulty solving equations (mathematical intelligence). For an interactive explanation of Gardner's work that students may also find interesting, go to the PBS website *Beta Thirteen WNET New York* at www.thirteen.org/ and search for "multiple intelligences."

Following is a brief explanation of each of the intelligences.

- Linguistic intelligence involves sensitivity to spoken and written language, the ability to learn languages, and the ability to use language effectively.
- Logical-mathematical intelligence involves skills in analyzing problems logically, carrying out mathematical operations, or investigating issues scientifically.

- Musical intelligence involves skills in performance, composition, and appreciation of musical patterns.
- Bodily-kinesthetic intelligence involves using one's whole body or parts of the body to solve problems.
- Spatial intelligence involves the ability to use patterns of wide space in confined areas.
- Interpersonal intelligence involves the capacity to understand others, their intentions, motivations, and desires.
- Intrapersonal intelligence involves the ability to understand oneself.
- Naturalist intelligence involves the ability to recognize, categorize, and draw upon certain features of the environment (Smith, 2002, 2008).

It is important for teachers to be aware of their students' predominant intelligences as they guide them in becoming independent learners while helping them meld their own intelligence with those of their classmates. For additional information, teachers may want to read Gardner's paper presented at the American Educational Research Association in 2003, "Multiple Intelligences After Twenty Years," posted on www.howardgardner.com.

Teaching with Multiple Intelligences and Multimodal Literacies

Gardner's work supports the concept of multimodal literacies, the integration of multiple modes of communication and expression. According to the National Council of Teachers of English's guideline on multimodal literacies, the use of different modes of expression in student work should be integrated into the overall literacy goals of the curriculum. These might include art, music, movement, and drama as well as digital literacies. What would learning look like that pairs multimodal literacies with an understanding of multiple intelligences?

In a unit on "oceans" in science or geography, for example, students may be grouped according to their predominant intelligences and given a task that utilizes their strengths. Students would then be "jigsawed," or rearranged so that students representing each intelligence would be grouped together to share their learning. This example can be adapted for any grade level.

- Linguistic students may find or write poems that express the poet's feelings about the ocean. They may also read short stories, essays, or novels related to the ocean, such as *Dove*, the true story of a young man who sailed around the world alone (Graham & Gill, 1991).
- Mathematical students may draw and explain a bathymetric profile of an ocean floor or create a chart showing sediment deposition rates.
- Musical students may explain echo sounding used for determining the depth of water and show how sound waves are used in other, everyday, ways. They may also bring in music or lyrics related to ocean themes.
- Spatial and kinesthetic students may work together to explain the physics of surfing as they demonstrate how wave energy is used to propel the surfboard forward as the surfer balances the trajectory of the board.
- Interpersonal students may facilitate small-group learning, acting as discussion directors. They might create questions related to each of the other modalities in an effort to go deeper, assisting students as they engage in productive dialogue.
- Intrapersonal students may examine human impact on oceans by creating writing prompts or role-playing activities, such as a newscast on how industrial pollution in oceans will impact life on Earth in the future.
- Naturalists may research and create a PowerPoint that depicts the habitats of organisms living in various marine ecosystems.

This type of group learning highlights students' innate abilities, fostering an intellectual synergy that can expand content-area reading miles beyond the textbook.

INTEGRATING CONCEPTS

Engagement in reading and learning may be difficult to define, but it is easy to spot in a classroom, although it may take different forms according to the type of texts, the specific group of students, or the learning environment. Unlike many of the initiatives that are mandated in schools, it is not systematic, scripted, or assessed by checklists. Although it may not suddenly appear in response to our entreaties, engagement can be nurtured by helping students become interested in a topic, giving them an authentic and relevant purpose for reading, and allowing them some autonomy in the learning task. Guthrie and Anderson (1999) remind us that "Students who read for involvement, curiosity, challenge, importance, and self-efficacy spend more time reading books than students who read for recognition, grades, competition, and compliance with the demands of a program" (p. 24). If we, as teachers, continue to focus on engagement as the "bullseye" in content-area reading, we will be successful in helping students become independent, self-determined learners.

Principles for Engagement

- Create (or have students create) an environment that immerses them in the topic of study by utilizing print-centric as well as visual texts such as photographs, maps, primary documents, videos, and online sites.
- Demonstrate for students how you, as a proficient subject-area reader, make meaning from texts.
- Allow students to try out new learning in a safe environment where mistakes are seen as an acceptable, if not necessary, component of learning.
- Teach students what it means to be an active rather than a passive reader.
- Give students some choice in texts, assignments, groups, and due dates.
- Contribute to students' self-efficacy by showing them that you know and care about them as individuals as well as learners.
- Use a variety of assessments, such as relevant and meaningful projects, presentations, and portfolios. Provide ongoing feedback for revision rather than relying only on final, summative assessments.
- Teach students about multiple intelligences and incorporate multimodal literacies in activities, projects and assignments.

Quote for Reflection

"One must be an inventor to read well."

—Ralph Waldo Emerson, "The American Scholar," 1837

Study Group Resources

Guthrie, J. T., & Alvermann, D. E. (Eds.). (1999). *Engaged reading: Processes, practices, and policy implications* (pp. 17–45). New York: Teachers College Press.

Kornhaber, M., Fierros, E., & Veenema, S. (2004). *Multiple intelligences: Best ideas from research and practice.* Needham Heights, MA: Prentice-Hall.

Lent, R. (2006). *Engaging adolescent learners: A guide for content-area teachers.* Portsmouth, NH: Heinemann.

Wilhelm, J. (2007). *Engaging readers and writers with inquiry: Promoting deep understanding in language arts and the content areas with guiding questions.* New York: Scholastic.

CHAPTER 2

Building Background for Reading

IN A WORKSHOP I WAS RECENTLY facilitating with content-area teachers, I asked participants the difference between engagement and motivation. A middle school teacher who apparently had experience with both answered, "Motivation is when kids want to do something; engagement is when they want to keep doing it." I loved the spontaneous definition, but it occurred to me later that our chances of motivating kids initially or engaging them for the long haul are pretty slim if they have insufficient background to connect to the topic of study.

Inherent in virtually all comprehension is the prior knowledge that each reader brings to the text. Prior knowledge, often referred to as background knowledge, is a part of our schema, the compilation of our unique thoughts and attitudes about a subject (Anderson & Pearson, 1984). Take, for example, the phrase "State Fair." My schema may be completely different from yours as I visualize going to a fair with my parents when I was very young. I have various compartments that contain my own knowledge and emotions regarding a fair, such as the rides with my associated fear of heights, the animals that I desperately wanted to touch, the magical smell of cotton candy and its disappointing, empty taste. You get the idea. When we learn, we connect new information to that which is already stored in our brains, forming a network of knowledge. If there is nothing for the new information to attach to, it is far less meaningful and relevant—and far more difficult to learn. In fact, some researchers cite prior knowledge as a "prerequisite to comprehending new information . . . imperative to the advancement of conceptual knowledge" (Guthrie & Anderson, 1999, p. 31). Sharon Kane is succinct in her assessment:

> The importance of background knowledge, or prior knowledge, to reading comprehension and to learning in general cannot be overstated. Researchers have found that readers spend up to 70 percent of their time interpreting the author's ideas and deciding how those ideas relate to their own prior knowledge on the subject. (2003, p. 97)

The problem is that students come to each class with individual ranges and depths of background knowledge. If a student has taken a trip to the Grand Canyon, for example, she has a mental picture of what sedimentary rocks look like and the power of erosion to alter Earth's physical features. This firsthand information will help her conceptualize other ideas in geology that her peers who have not had such experiences may have difficulty understanding. Background knowledge also works as a magnet to attract more knowledge. Students who have seen the glass-encased pillow stained with Lincoln's dried blood at the Petersen House in Washington, D.C., may develop a keen interest in Abraham Lincoln and events surrounding his life, most notably the Civil War. Such interest may lead them to watch Ken Burns's video *The Civil War* (1990), read historical novels set during the Civil War such as *Cold Mountain* (Frazier, 2006), and take a greater interest when studying this time period. It may also help students think more critically about war in general as they begin to make connections from the Civil War to other conflicts or from Lincoln to recent presidents who have held the office during wartime or been assassinated.

Although teachers cannot possibly even the background knowledge playing field, they can assess and then activate students' prior knowledge by linking what they are learning to what they already know. This is especially helpful before introducing them to a new subject. Following are instructional practices that will activate background knowledge and help students make generative connections.

BRAINSTORMING FOR BACKGROUND KNOWLEDGE

Although brainstorming has been used for years in business to come up with creative jingles in advertising or new body designs in car manufacturing, variations of this popular technique can also be used by teachers to tap into students' prior knowledge. In an English, history, or Latin class, for instance, before reading *The Odyssey* (Homer, 2006), place students in small groups with a sheet of chart paper containing an important word or phrase from *The Odyssey* such as "Cyclops," "Ulysses," or "voyage." Allow students no more than 5 minutes to brainstorm everything they know about the term before passing the chart to another group. The next round of brainstorming will build on what the previous group listed, and then the paper will be passed to another group. Charts can be placed on classroom walls and new information or illustrations added as students read, creating a "Velcro" effect to help new learning stick.

Use the same activity to deepen thinking with questions such as "What is the most important voyage a person can take in his or her lifetime?" or "Which obligation is more important: to protect one's country and risk death, or to support the family by being there with them?"

There are endless varieties of brainstorming activities to help students make connections, such as having students freewrite or draw what they know about hydrogen atoms in science, for example, or polynomials in geometry before, during, or after study. Students will compose and then pass their papers to the student on their left in a circle. They will then have a few minutes to respond to the writer's comments or drawing. The passing continues until four students have replied to the original posting. Students enjoy reading what their "blog" initiated, and classmates' comments expand one another's knowledge in the process.

ACTIVATING BACKGROUND KNOWLEDGE THROUGH PREDICTION GUIDES

Anticipation or prediction guides (Herber, 1978) not only assess what students know but also guide dialogue, deepen understanding, and challenge beliefs. In *PreReading Activities for Content Area Reading and Learning,* the authors note that anticipation guides enhance comprehension by encouraging students to focus attention on concepts in the text while arousing their curiosity. They go on to describe how effective guides can create a "mismatch" between prior knowledge and new learning. When students read, they attempt to resolve these differences, giving them a purpose for reading and activating their prior knowledge. The authors make the reasonable argument that unactivated prior knowledge is useless (Readence, Moore, & Rickelman, 2000).

When developing a prediction guide, create questions or statements that require deep thinking, not low-level questions that can be easily answered by locating facts in the text. Also, include items that tap into students' beliefs or emotions, even those that might ignite controversy. Discuss students' responses and then use the guides to set a purpose for reading. Students will interact with the text as they read to confirm, revise, or change their answers. Prediction guides can also be used as prompts for discussion prior to reading. Below are samples of anticipation guides for various subject areas.

- Agree/Disagree Prediction Guide for Science

   Topic: Selective Breeding

   Directions: Circle "Agree" or "Disagree" based on your opinion of each statement.

   1. Genetically engineering plants to increase productivity of food for humans is ethically irresponsible.

      Agree   Disagree

2. Purebred dogs can exhibit harmful traits because of inbreeding.

    Agree   Disagree

- Open-ended Prediction Guide for English

    Topic: Young adult novel for literature circles: *Uglies* (Westerfeld, 2005).

    Directions: Answer each question based on your own beliefs. There is no right or wrong answer.

    1. What does it mean to be beautiful?

    2. If you could have an operation to make you physically beautiful, but you would look very similar to every one else, would you opt to have the operation? Why or why not?

- Discussion Prediction Guide for Social Studies (or before reading the young adult novel *Crossing the Wire* (Hobbs, 2007).

    Topic: Government and People of Mexico/Immigration

    Directions: Elect a discussion direction and recorder. In small groups, discuss everything you know about Mexico. The recorder will make note of the group's talking points.

    Mexico's government

    Mexico's people

    Mexico's food

    Mexico and immigration

    Mexico and North American Free Trade Agreement (NAFTA)

- Prediction Guide for Algebra

    Topic: Inequalities

    Directions: Read the word problem. You don't need to find the answer. Just complete the sentences below the problem, explaining what you would do first and then next to begin to solve this problem.

You have a friend, Bill, who lives 3 miles from
school, and another friend, Mary, who lives 2 miles
from the same school. You want to estimate the
distance that separates their homes.

First, I would _____.

Then, I would _____.

BUILDING BACKGROUND KNOWLEDGE THROUGH DIALOGUE

Dialogue has been at the center of the American experience since
the founding of our country. While we once gathered in taverns
to discuss how we could free ourselves of English rule, we now
gather at the water cooler in offices, at our kids' ballgames, or
in churches to talk about the price of gasoline, peace talks in the
Middle East, or how we can help those who have survived a natural disaster. It is through such talk that we come to understand
events that affect our lives, adding relevant "hypertexts" to our
schema. Students need the same opportunities to internalize and
adapt what they are learning in school and in the world at large. If
students spend the majority of their class time listening to lectures,
answering questions, or taking notes from textbooks, they may be
losing a valuable opportunity to increase their knowledge through
verbal interaction.

Increasing Comprehension through Dialogue

In a report titled "Academic Literacy Instruction for Adolescents," five recommendations are provided for improving adolescents' reading comprehension, including "Increase the amount and
quality of open, sustained discussion of reading content." The authors explain, "Students who have repeated opportunities to explore
the meaning of text in discussions with their teachers or peers develop habits of analysis and critical thinking that support improved
comprehension when they read text on their own" (Torgesen et al.,
2007, p. 38). Brown and Campaione's study found that discussion
helps students "evaluate, integrate, and elaborate knowledge in
new ways" (cited in Guthrie & Anderson, 1999, p. 36).

Dialogue also increases comprehension by helping students dig deeper into the text, experience shifts in understanding, and gain insights that they may not be able to attain individually. The idea of collective wisdom has been the topic of several recent books and articles, both for educators and for business, such as James Surowiecki's bestselling *The Wisdom of Crowds*. His premise, that groups are often smarter than the smartest people in them, is convincing and has implications for classroom practices. Surowiecki's definition of *wise crowds* includes four factors: diversity of opinion, independence of members from one another, decentralization, and a good method for aggregating opinions. Teachers can use these conditions to create discussions that will help students experience the collective wisdom of a knowledgeable and focused group.

Activities and Resources for Fostering Dialogue

Following are activities and resources that can support students as they learn to become effective participants in dialogue.

- Write several quotes on the board related to the topic and ask students to choose a quote they want to discuss with a partner. For example, in a psychology or biology class, students could respond to a quote from the magazine *Scientific American Mind:* "Research shows that females may have an advantage when it comes to episodic memory, a type of long-term memory based on personal experiences" (Branan, 2008, p. 7). Give students a few minutes at the beginning or end of the period for partner or small-group discussion.
- Allow students to engage in debates, letter discussions (where they write to one another before speaking), forums, or online chats. Include questions that require students to take sides on an issue and defend their positions. For example, before high school students read Steinbeck's *Of Mice and Men* (2002), engage them in a debate on euthanasia, perhaps bringing in an article about Dr. Kevorkian to stimulate discussion and build background information before reading. Encourage students to change their positions if they are convinced to do so.
- Before studying a specific topic, find an interesting connection for students to consider. For example, when

introducing students to the Fibonacci sequence in geometry or science, ask them to discuss how it was used as a clue in *The Da Vinci* Code (Brown, 2006). Students in math can also listen to *The Math Guy* on National Public Radio (http://www.stanford.edu/~kdevlin/MathGuy.html) and discuss his real-world connections to mathematical principles.

- Create seminars or forums by having students read about current issues and facilitate discussions among their classmates—or an even larger audience. In one school, students organized and led a community forum on banned books during the American Library Association's banned book week (www.ala.org).

- The National Issues Forum (www.nifi.org) offers resources on how to structure a forum on a variety of topics ranging from economic issues to energy and the environment. You can order materials from the website that explain the nature of deliberative discourse as well as booklets that provide pro and con arguments on controversial issues. The National Paideia Center also provides resources for fostering democratic dialogue through seminars that use open-ended questions to facilitate understanding of texts. A sample seminar plan for the "Gettysburg address" can be found on their website, www.paideia.org.

Begin the process of creating a dialogue-centered classroom by assessing the type of interaction that is already taking place in your class.

- Do the questions you ask elicit discussion?
- Is there often an open dialogue, a free exchange of information among students?
- Do students feel free to express opinions about topics?
- Do you encourage students to "piggy-back" on others' comments to expand dialogue?

As you try the exercises described above, how does the level of dialogue change? Once students understand that they are expected to be active participants in the learning community, the environment will reflect the excitement of an animated discussion.

INTEGRATING CONCEPTS

Building and activating students' background knowledge is a wise investment of your curricular time and energy. Students' increased engagement and conceptual understanding will become evident as relevant connections reinforce new learning. Much like preparing the soil before planting a garden, the richness of background knowledge will create the most balanced environment for optimal, sustained growth.

Principles for Building Background

- Take sufficient time to access, activate, and build students' background knowledge about a topic before beginning its study.
- Use a variety of brainstorming activities to help students make connections before, during, and after reading.
- Create anticipation or prediction guides to assess prior knowledge, set a purpose for reading, challenge beliefs, and arouse students' curiosity.
- Incorporate discussion into content-area study to support analysis and critical thinking while expanding background knowledge.

Quote for Reflection

"One place comprehended can make us understand other places better."

—Eudora Welty, 1979

Study Group Resources

Copeland, M. (2005). *Socratic circles: Fostering critical and creative thinking in middle and high school.* Portland, ME: Stenhouse.

Marzano, R. (2004). *Building background knowledge for academic achievement: Research on what works in schools.* Alexandria, VA: Association for Supervision and Curriculum Development.

Readence, J. E., Moore, D. W., & Rickelman, R. J. (2000). *Pre-reading activities for content-area reading and learning* (3rd ed.). Newark, DE: International Reading Association.

CHAPTER 3

Making Meaning through Reading

CONTENT-AREA TEACHERS OFTEN get excited about their subjects and can create spontaneous learning communities for their peers, as well as for interested students. Sit with a group of teachers of economics or government, for instance, and you may hear predictions about the future of Social Security, discussions about how one can be fiscally conservative yet socially liberal, and detailed analyses about the Federal Reserve Board's decisions to raise or lower the prime interest rate. Science teachers can be equally passionate about microorganisms, theories about global warming, and, especially, new lab equipment. English teachers can pack an hour-long book discussion into a 20-minute lunch. And on it goes through the rather tightly knit departments of most secondary schools. This passion generally works to inspire students, especially when the topic calls for engaging activities or project-based learning. Such passion may hit a wall of resistance, however, when teachers ask students to read texts to gain understandings that support activities. Sometimes even exemplary teachers with a high level of expertise give up the battle to "make" kids read both textbooks and supplemental assignments, finding alternative ways of relaying core information through PowerPoint presentations, lectures, videos, or even by reading aloud to students. When this happens, students often fail to comprehend important content-area knowledge and risk falling behind in essential, domain-specific reading skills.

READING IN THE CONTENT AREA

It is true that most subject-area teachers have not been trained as reading teachers, and they should not be expected to provide intensive reading instruction, but an important part of their role in helping students understand content is to teach them how to read proficiently within their disciplines. A 2007 document from the Alliance for Excellent Education titled *Literacy Instruction in the Content Areas: Getting to the Core of Middle and High School Improvement* (Heller & Greenleaf, 2007) specifically addresses content-area learning rather than the generic reading strategies that have been at the forefront of staff development in recent years. The report quotes the National Center for Education and the Economy (NCEE): "This is a world in which a very high level of preparation in reading, writing, speaking, mathematics, science, literature, history, and the arts will be an indispensable foundation for everything that comes after for most members of the workforce" (NCEE, 2006). The notion of "reading across the curriculum" is no longer enough. Teachers must address the literacy demands that are *specific* to their content areas because studies have shown that literacy skills are not easily transferred from one content area to another (Alvermann & Moore, 1991).

Consider how drawing references, an important skill for comprehension, can be taught differently in various domains. In a 10th-grade English class, for example, students may study the first stanza of Jimmy Santiago Baca's poem, "I Am Offering This Poem."

I am offering this poem to you,
Since I have nothing else to give.
Keep it like a warm coat
When winter comes to cover you,
Or like a pair of thick socks
The cold cannot bite through.

Students must understand metaphor, the role of the poem's speaker, and tone to infer the poet's message accurately.

Now look at the skills that are necessary for these same 10th-grade students in a social studies class to draw an inference about the political cartoon in Figure 3.1.

Drawing an inference from this cartoon requires the student to have sufficient background knowledge to understand the message as well as the purpose of political cartoons, the cartoonist's stance, and the symbolic significance of the man and children. Further, the teacher may engage students in a discussion about racial or ethnic inferences implied by the cartoonist's choice of "characters."

Figure 3.2, from NASA's website, http://data.giss.nasa.gov/gistemp/graphs/, requires that 10th-grade science students understand the basics of reading a graph, know the definition of "mean" as it is used in this context, and be able to apply the information from the written text to the graph to draw an accurate inference.

FIGURE 3.1. Political SUV Cartoon

Reprinted by permission of Cagle Cartoons.

Figure 3.2. Global Annual Mean Surface Air Temperature Change

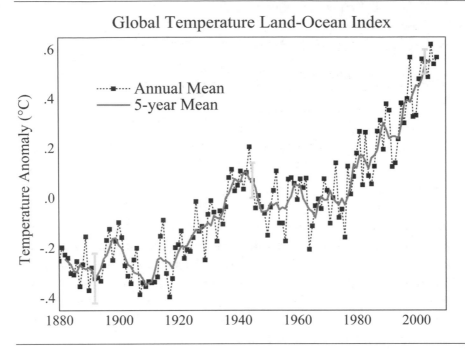

Global Temperature Land-Ocean Index

Source: NASA.

So, explaining to students that drawing an inference is "reading between the lines" and teaching them generic "inferencing" strategies will do little to advance their content knowledge. Instead, teachers can ensure that their students know how to comprehend texts and media in various disciplines by showing them how mathematicians, scientists, historians, or poets read, write, and think.

RECOGNIZING TEXT STRUCTURE

When students first approach text—whether the text is a novel, a primary document such as a photograph or letter, an explanation in a science textbook about chemical bonding, or a website from the Library of Congress—their comprehension will increase if they understand how the author structured the text to convey meaning. The RAND Reading Study Group (2003) determined that students who can identify text structures increase not only their comprehension but also their recall. Figure 3.3 defines the most common types of text structure.

Think about the numerous types of texts, each with varying text structures, that students read throughout their school day. To add to the confusion, text structures with the same name may look completely different in each class. "Problem and solution" in a math class, for example, is straightforward and unambiguous, with both symbols and words delivering the text. In science, "problem and solution" may be anything but straightforward, with a myriad of interlocking problems and solutions, such as when reading about cures for diseases. In English, "problem and solution" may take the shape of a fantasy creature in a young adult novel who must find a way to save his tribe from extinction. In history, "problem and solution" is subject to interpretation according to the individual recounting the problem or solution, often through primary documents. Just as with the example regarding drawing inferences earlier in the chapter, teaching students generic text structures and how they are signaled by certain words or phrases is not enough to help students become proficient readers in various content areas.

Using Text Structure to Increase Comprehension

One of the most effective ways to help students use text structure to aid comprehension is by showing them how and why the author has organized text in a certain way in your domain. Following are activities to help students with this important skill.

FIGURE 3.3. Text Structure: Types and Characteristics

Types of Text Structures	Characteristics
Narration	Setting, plot, characters, theme, sequential and nonsequential organization
Cause-Effect	Explains *why* actions or events happen
Problem-Solution	Shows one or more solutions to one or more problems
Compare-Contrast	Shows how two or more things are alike (compare) or different (contrast)
Description	Explains event, place, person, idea, or concept
Enumeration	Explains broad concepts through specific facts or examples
Sequence	Shows events in the order in which they happen
Argument	Promotes a supposition supported with facts

- Give students a copy of the chart in Figure 3.3. Have them preview the assigned text with a partner and, after determining the text structure, discuss why the author used a certain structure to convey meaning. How might the "message" change with a different organizational pattern? Ask students if one type of text structure is easier for them to comprehend than others, and if so, why.
- Show students how to use nonprint features of a text, such as graphs, illustrations, maps, or cartoons. In textbooks, have students attend to words in bold or captions, and show them how these features support the text structure. An 8th-grade text on the solar system, for instance, includes an illustration showing the stages of the solar system's formation, an example of sequence as well as of cause and effect.
- Read aloud articles or passages from your discipline, showing students how writers in your field organize text to enhance meaning. P.E. teachers can assist in this area by reading sports articles to students (or showing them video clips of sports reports) and pointing out how the writer organizes the text, often with an exciting bit of narration to begin the article and then moving into description or cause and effect in explaining the actions of the players. Have students examine the article to see if the text structure led the reader to favor one team or player over another.
- Have students change headings in textbooks to questions and then read to answer the questions, paying attention to how text structure is an organizational tool to show readers what is more, or less, important. For example, in a chemistry text about water molecules where a heading reads "Cohesion and Adhesion," students could change the heading into a question such as: How do cohesion and adhesion compare or contrast?
- Show videos related to your subject, such as *Into the Wild* (2007), *A Beautiful Mind* (2001), or *Troy* (2004), and discuss how the screenplay writer used text structure to organize events and construct meaning.

Understanding Text Structure through Graphic Organizers

Graphic organizers are tools that present a systematic, visual representation of the text. Their advantages in helping students comprehend and think critically are well documented (Alvermann, 1986). Students who use graphic organizers appropriately begin to understand the structure of texts and see how ideas are related as they "receive, organize, and evaluate information so that it makes sense to them" (Irvin, Buehl, & Klemp, 2003).

In *Classroom Instruction That Works* (Marzano, Pickering, & Pollock, 2001), the authors devote an entire chapter to the six types of graphic organizers that they contend represent the most common patterns into which most information is organized: descriptive, time-sequence, process/cause–effect, episode, generalization/principle, and concept. Adapt organizers in this book or go to one of the many online sites that offer free graphic organizers, such as www.graphicorganizers.com, and provide students with a variety of blank graphic organizers. Have students choose one that is appropriate to what they are reading and then share with a small group how the organizer enhanced their understanding of the text. In a seventh-grade geography or science class, for instance, students could use a graphic organizer such as the one in Figure 3.4 to help them see how specific facts or examples increase their knowledge of the Kalahari Desert.

Students could then take each of the facts about the Kalahari and create another graphic organizer that shows the structure the writer used to expand that particular fact. For example, a cause-and-effect map would show the effects of modern civilization on the desert's natural resources. A Venn diagram would compare and contrast the animal population in the Kalahari with that of the Sahara.

FIGURE 3.4. Graphic Organizer for Kalahari Desert

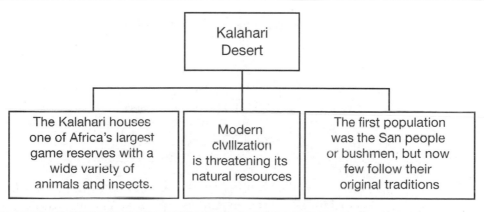

Understanding Text Structure through Picture Books

In an article titled "Picture Books for Young Adult Readers" (2001), author Sunya Osborn explains that picture books are useful tools for demonstrating important reading skills such as inferring, visualizing, determining importance, and developing background knowledge. My own experience with picture books in secondary classes confirms Osborn's observations. In fact, over the past decade, a new trend in picture books for older readers, often called "crossovers," has transformed the concept of such books as texts that are only for children. "Picture books can enhance content of learners of any age. They appeal to visual learners, integrate the arts, and provide background and a context to focus on a theme" (Carr, Buchannan, Wentz, Weiss, & Brant, 2001, p. 149).

Picture books are also valuable resources in helping students identify and understand text structure while exposing them to a wide range of exceptionally engaging visual text. The following picture books can be used as prompts for discussing specific text structures.

- Cause and Effect
    Alverez, J. (2000). *The Secret Footprints*
    Popov, N. (1995). *Why?* (visual text only; no words)

- Problem/Solution
    Nivola, C. (2008). *Planting the Trees of Kenya: The Story of Wangari Maathai*
    Deedy, C. A. (2000). *The Yellow Star: The Legend of King Christian X of Denmark*

- Compare/Contrast
    Nikola-Lisa, W. (2006). *How We are Smart*
    Smith, C. R., Jr. (2007). *Twelve Rounds to Glory: The Story of Muhammad Ali*

- Description
    Myers, W. D. (2002). *Patrol: An American Soldier in Vietnam*
    Bunting, E. (1999). *Smoky Night*

- Sequence
    Myers, W. D. (2003). *Malcolm X: A Fire Burning Brightly*
    Borden, L. (2004). *Sea Clocks: The Story of Longitude*

- Narration
  Deedy, C. A. (2007). *Martina, the Beautiful Cockroach: A Cuban Folktale* (also in Spanish)
  Tompert, A. (2003). *Joan of Arc: Heroine of France*

DETERMINING IMPORTANCE

Give students a handout and ask them to highlight what's important. You'll soon see entire pages lighting up in fluorescent pink or yellow. Determining what is important in a text is a difficult skill that many adults continue to refine, yet it is essential for making inferences, summarizing, synthesizing, and understanding logic and argument. In fact, one of the hallmarks of proficient readers is that they can distinguish important information from irrelevant or unimportant information in a text (Keen & Zimmermann, 2007). Determining importance also depends on your purpose (Irvin, Buehl, & Klemp, 2003). If you lose your cellphone and you have a protection plan, you will read the document differently than if you are reading to gain an overall understanding of the provisions of your plan.

Although no one would deny that students must independently learn to determine what is most important in a text, our test-driven, fast-paced curriculum often denies students the opportunity for practicing this skill. When students are reading to determine what a teacher will ask on a test, for example, they are only trying to figure out someone else's interpretation of importance. Instead, we must give students many occasions to assume responsibility in practicing and refining this skill.

Determining Importance through Out-of-School Literacies

Deciding what is important in a text will not suddenly be mastered, as standardized test–makers would have us believe. It is, instead, a skill that varies according to the subject, the purpose, the text, and the student's background knowledge. Teachers act as guides, but students must ultimately find their own direction as independent learners. One way to show students how to determine importance is by helping them transfer their out-of-school literacies to subject-area reading. Use questions such as the following to guide a discussion about how determining importance is a part of everyday life.

1. When you read a videogame manual, what are you looking for? What is important?
2. When you listen to a long message on your cellphone or someone gives you directions to a new place, what do you write down?
3. When you watch a movie, what parts of the movie do you decide to relate to friends? How do you determine what you will share instead of retelling the entire plot?
4. If you read a blog or an entry on Facebook, what do you skim? What do you slow down and read carefully? How do you determine what is worth reading?
5. When you read a sports article or an online news article, what are you looking for?
6. When you listen to the lyrics of a song or see an advertisement, what sticks with you?
7. In what way does the purpose for determining what is important affect your interpretation of what is important?

Before students read an assigned text, talk about why you are having them read the text and ask what they want to learn. Take the necessary time to show relevance to their lives and interests. If you can't make a case for relevance, consider skipping the topic entirely. Teaching one concept in depth that students can internalize, use, and adapt to other learning is far more valuable than covering a series of topics superficially. Groups of teachers who teach the same subject may want to reexamine their curriculum in light of relevance and make important decisions about what needs to be taught in depth and how they can allow students to assume responsibility for determining what is important. For example, in an English class, students can divide into groups to study a particular poet's works rather than superficially covering a series of poems by various poets.

Determining Importance through Interactive Practices

Following are activities that will help students become aware of what is important as they read.

*   Provide photographs for students to analyze. The Oakland Museum of California has an extensive online collection of Dorothea Lange's photographs of immigrants and those living during the Depression:

http://www.oac.cdlib.org/. *Photo by Brady: A Picture of the Civil War* (Armstrong, 2005), a book for adolescents that presents stark Civil War photographs with accompanying text, is also a good resource. Have students analyze the photographs' importance by discussing the following questions:

> If someone is looking for pictures of a relative, what would be important in the photographs?
>
> If someone is trying to determine the impact of the Great Depression or war on children, what would be important to observe?
>
> If someone felt that the photographs had been staged as a propaganda tool, what details would be important to note?
>
> What might the subject of the photograph say was important about the image? The photographer?

- Have students examine political cartoons to determine what background knowledge is essential to "get" the message. Students enjoy bringing in cartoons and posting them on a "Do You Get It?" bulletin board. The *New Yorker's Book of Political Cartoons* (Mankoff & Buckley, 2000) contains smart cartoons depicting a wide variety of topics. Political cartoons can also be found in most newspapers and many current events magazines as well as online. Take a look at www.politicalcartoons.com. Have students create a two-column organizer to use as they read. In the left column, students will list important facts or ideas needed to "get" the cartoon, and in the right column they will explain why the fact is important. Have students work in small groups to compare their lists.
- Have students create their own graphic organizers that demonstrate creative ways of notating the main idea and supporting details in texts.
- Allow students to work with a partner or in a small group to discuss what is most important in a chapter, article, photograph, chart, short story, poem, or novel. This activity is also useful when students are working through word problems. Students can add their contribution to a "What's Important" chart for articles related to science or

social studies topics and then share their talking points with the entire class.

- Indulge students in their fondness for sticky notes. They can use different colors to denote what they feel is more and less important.
- Have students set a purpose for their reading, or set one for them, to help them engage with the text and increase comprehension. For example, have students read an article from *Newsweek* about the economy with the following purpose: "Read to find out how the economy can be influenced by people's beliefs in its strength or weakness" or "Read to determine if you agree that a significant factor in a worsening economy is people's lack of trust in its stability."
- When possible, provide activities that allow students to express their understanding of importance in various ways. Give opportunities for writing, drawing, discussing, and role-playing or for using multimodal literacies, such as websites or digital video composing before, during, and after reading. Remember that engagement is a key component of deep learning.

GENERATING QUESTIONS

Comprehension means building understanding. We teach students how to engage actively in understanding text by dissecting, probing, interpreting, analyzing, synthesizing, summarizing, and questioning. In *Improving Comprehension with Questioning the Author* (2006), Beck and McKeown explain how teachers' queries can enhance comprehension through a process that develops the meaning of ideas in the course of reading.

> Queries . . . are designed to change the role of the teacher from quiz-show host to discussion facilitator. A teacher who uses queries focuses less on evaluating student responses and more on encouraging students to consider an author's ideas and to respond to one another's interpretations of those ideas. (p. 36)

Further, when students generate questions based on what they are reading, they grapple with meaning. This process contrasts with mechanically following a school-generated script of answering test questions, turning them over for a grade, and moving on to the next set of questions, often without truly understanding the content or retaining what is important.

Generating Meaningful Questions

Help students investigate for meaning by demonstrating the difference between low-level questions, such as "What is a vaccine?"—a question that requires little explanation, and more thoughtful questions such as "How do vaccines prevent diseases? What are the risks? How would you weigh the risk of vaccinating your child against common childhood diseases and the possibility of the child's developing a permanent disability?"

Marie Clay's work with young children supports using this instructional practice with older students. She encourages teachers to allow students to take responsibility for the learning process and work independently as they discover new things "inside and outside the lesson." Clay refers to such learning as "pushing the boundaries" of students' knowledge, leading to independence and deep learning (2002, p. 13). Teaching students to read as investigators is an effective way to help them push their own boundaries and develop a sense of personal agency. For example, if students in a high school English or social studies class are reading Patricia McCormick's *Sold* (2008), a powerful novel about a young girl in India who is sold into prostitution, you could show them the difference between traditional study-guide questions and higher-level, critical-thinking questions such as in Figure 3.5. Using your questions as a model, have students create their own questions; what do *they* consider important?

FIGURE 3.5. Questions for *Sold*

Low-Level Questions for *Sold*	Critical-Thinking Questions for *Sold*
Why was Lakshmi sold into prostitution?	What, if anything, could Lakshmi have done to prevent what happened to her?
Where was the novel set?	How might things have been different if Lakshmi's society allowed her mother to have more power in the family?
Who is Mutmaz?	Do you believe that Mutmaz's character is based on a real person? Explain.

Activities for Generating Meaningful Questions

Other activities for helping students generate questions include the following:

- Place students with partners or in small groups to create and then debate questions. Post the questions as prompts for whole-class dialogue with students facilitating the discussions.
- Have students create comic strips or mini–graphic novels that turn questions into the theme of the comic. For example, how did the American Chestnut Blight destroy virtually all of the Chestnut trees during the early 1900s? How can the Pythagorean theorem be used to solve everyday problems? Go to www.comicbookproject.org or *Building Literacy Connections with Graphic Novels: Page by Page, Panel by Panel* (Carter, 2007) for other ideas regarding graphic novels and comic books.
- Allow students to role-play as journalists, asking questions of a classmate who will act as an expert on the topic or a text.
- Have students create a question "exit slip" that they will hand to you or exchange with another student as they leave class. You may also have students create questions for "entrance slips" as they come into class.
- Talk to students about the fallibilities inherent in text, especially online text. Encourage them to read skeptically and critically with question marks rather than periods in their minds. See http://www.philb.com/fakesites.htm for examples of fake or spoof websites. Chapter 6 contains additional information about reading online sites critically.

INTEGRATING CONCEPTS

Through deep and thoughtful reading, the student and the text become engaged in a dance of meaning. Ultimately, each student must discover his or her own moves as you, the coach, demonstrate, guide, correct, and provide the music.

Principles for Reading for Meaning

- Teach students how text structure can facilitate understanding in your subject area.

- Provide graphic organizers to help students identify text structure and understand its role in making meaning.
- Use picture books for older students to demonstrate text structure.
- Help students determine what is important in a text by transferring the skills they use every day to your subject area.
- Provide multiple opportunities for students to determine importance in a variety of texts.
- Show students how to generate critical-thinking questions that get at the deeper meaning of a text by providing models that encourage them to create and answer their own questions.

Quote for Reflection

"What is reading, but silent conversation."

—Charles Lamb, critic, poet, and essayist

Study Group Resources

Beck, I. L., & McKeown, M. G. (2006). *Improving comprehension with questioning the author: A fresh and expanded view of a powerful approach.* New York: Scholastic.

Kane, S. (2003). *Literacy learning in the content areas.* Scottsdale, AZ: Holcomb Hathaway.

Tovani, C. (2004). *Do I really have to teach reading? Content comprehension 6–12.* Portland, ME: Stenhouse.

CHAPTER 4

Vocabulary:
The Key to Meaning

CARL SAGAN ONCE SAID, "It is of interest to note that some
dolphins are reported to have learned English—up to fifty
words used in correct context—no human being has been
reported to have learned dolphinese." Students don't learn dolphinese in content-area classes, of course, but they sometimes respond
to vocabulary study as if they are being asked to learn words used
by another species. Perhaps they feel overwhelmed by the number
of words they must learn for each of their classes, or perhaps they
don't gain sufficient conceptual knowledge about words to make
meaningful and long-lasting connections. In any event, vocabulary
continues to be one of the most complex components of content-
area reading.

At the same time, research over the past several years shows vocabulary to be the single most important factor contributing to reading comprehension (Billmeyer & Barton, 2002). In fact, vocabulary acquisition is absolutely essential to content-area studies. Students not only must have a broad body of word knowledge to acquire basic skills and become proficient readers, but they also need specialized vocabulary for many topics in classes such as math, science, and social studies.

CHALLENGES IN WORD STUDY

Teachers know students must learn topic-related words in order to grasp the concepts inherent in their content. Because the mastery of such words is so important, many teachers begin a new unit by handing out a list of words, sometimes a new list each week, and requiring that students memorize the words and their definitions. If we have learned anything over the past several decades, it is that only using a dictionary or glossary to learn words is an ineffective method of vocabulary study. While students may retain the definitions for the purpose of testing, they often fail to grasp the complex and interconnected meanings of words and phrases that form the foundation of content study. It takes time to build conceptual layers, but such construction is essential to deep and meaningful learning.

If it is true that vocabulary study is inexorably tied to reading, must students learn every word related to a unit of study? Because some words are essential to know and others are used infrequently, teachers should make informed decisions about whether the word is necessary for an understanding of the topic or if the word is a tag for a meaning that students may encounter less often. For example, the word *republic* is one that most agree should be a part of every history student's vocabulary bank, including how a republic works and in what ways it differs from a democracy or monarchy. The dictionary definition of *republic*—"political system with powerful electorate"—does not lend itself to in-depth understanding, nor does the secondary definition—"country with republican government." In fact, the second definition is one that could confuse students who may use their background knowledge to assume that when Republicans win an election, the government is a republic, but if Democrats win, it becomes a democracy. On the other hand, although the word *theocrat* should be defined, especially if students are studying theocracies, it would not necessarily be a word that needs to be firmly established in students' long-term memory. The point is that if all words are equally important, vocabulary study for most students will become discouraging, overwhelming, and, in some cases, counterproductive.

To add to the confusion, textbook publishers often list words that they deem important at the beginning of chapters or units, and many teachers use these lists inflexibly, perhaps believing that their students must know all of the words in order to learn a certain topic. Although these lists may be a starting point for studying a subject, they are certainly not a definitive guide for all students in all classes. For example, some students may have heard of many of the words, others may have studied the words in other classes or been exposed to them through personal experiences or reading, and still others may have no knowledge of the words at all. In addition, the teacher may determine that some of the words are too obscure, difficult, or unrelated to students' learning goals.

WORD STUDY BEFORE READING

To optimize word learning as well as instructional time, it is important to determine which words are necessary for students to learn deeply, which definitions simply should be provided, and which words may not be necessary to study at all. These decisions should be made based on your students' prior knowledge and the depth to which you plan to cover the content. While some teachers may feel uncomfortable with the amount of time it takes for word study prior to beginning a new unit or topic, this is actually *content* study, a type of intellectual soil preparation for what is to be planted.

When students are familiar with academic vocabulary before tackling the chapter, their understanding of the concepts within the chapter increases dramatically (Marzano, 2004). The goal is for students to move from being word definers to being word owners because when they learn words such as *bioengineering*, *tyranny*, or *theorem*, they learn content.

The notion of dividing words into tiers is explained by Beck, McKeown, and Kucan in *Bringing Words to Life* (2002). The chart in

FIGURE 4.1. Word Differentiation Chart

Vocabulary students should know already	Vocabulary students must learn for content understanding	Vocabulary students will encounter infrequently
labor	*sweatshop*	*Rose Cohen*
exploited	*child labor laws*	*Progressive Party*

Figure 4.1, an application of that research, demonstrates how teachers might "tier" words from a unit on child labor for an eighth-grade social studies class. Before introducing a topic to students, make a list of words that are related to the topic of study. Differentiate the words into the three categories, as shown in Figure 4.1.

Once you have sorted the words, assess your students' familiarity with them. The results may surprise you.

Write the words from your own units that appear in the first two columns on the board. Say the words for students in case they don't recognize the spelling of a word they may know. Then, provide a blank chart, such as the one in Figure 4.2. Ask students to copy the words from the board and place them in the left-hand column. They should then identify to what extent they know a word by placing a check in the appropriate column to its right.

Make sure students write their names on their charts but assure them that this type of assessment is *not* for a grade. After you review their assessment, differentiate instruction further based on students' prior knowledge. If none of the students knows the vocabulary, you will need to spend time developing understandings of the words by offering plenty of print-based and visual examples. Provide a variety of student-focused activities, such as having them sketch meanings of words, role-play, find words on the Internet,

FIGURE 4.2. Word Familiarity Chart

New Word	Know it well—can use it in a sentence	Think I might know it—might be able to guess at its meaning	Have heard it—but couldn't use it in a sentence or define it	Never heard it—have no idea what it means

or watch videos related to the vocabulary. In short, the more opportunities students have to hear, see, and use the words, the better they will understand the word and its associated concepts in your subject area.

If there are only a few students who don't know certain words, place them in groups with students who know the words and have them share their knowledge. Move from group to group, correcting misperceptions or inaccurate definitions. This exercise encourages students to pay attention to important words and creates a purpose for reading about them in upcoming study. It may be necessary for you to provide extra activities for students who lack prior knowledge about a topic or are English language learners. Because it is important for students to *experience* new vocabulary, this is a great opportunity for collaborative learning as students build broad, conceptual understandings of key terms.

For words in the third column of Figure 4.1 (words students will encounter infrequently), make sure the meanings are posted or that you provide a glossary sheet to allow students easy access to definitions. You may also want to provide background information to explain this vocabulary, while at the same time building an understanding of words in the first two columns. For example, you could briefly tell students the story of Rose Cohen, a young girl who began working in a sweatshop in 1892, without having them memorize her name or testing them on the facts of the story.

Once students have been introduced to content-area words, they are ready to add the next layer of understanding.

WORD STUDY DURING READING

Vocabulary study is an ongoing process, one that requires frequent attention and monitoring while students are reading. Many of the following activities also can be used before or after reading.

Making Connections

One way that we all remember new vocabulary is by making a personal connection to words. According to William Nagy in *Teaching Vocabulary to Improve Reading Comprehension* (2004), "The first property of powerful vocabulary instruction is integration—tying new words with familiar concepts and experiences" (p. 23). Have students create their own individual vocabulary logs to record words they don't know or can't remember, along with an explanation of the word and a connection they have made to the word. Such a connection may include synonyms, sentences, pictures, or graphics within the context to help reinforce the meaning. A sample "Word Connection Log" for a sixth-grade science class is provided in Figure 4.3.

Conceptualizing Words

While reading, students will begin to move from defining words to conceptualizing them. When students understand the concept behind the definition, such as the layered connotations surrounding the word *prejudice,* they are then ready to adapt and use the word in a variety of contexts. This process can be facilitated by having students create word maps, sometimes called concept or semantic maps, to assist them in thinking deeply about all aspects of the word (Heimlich & Pittelman, 1986). A typical word map places the word in the center and then asks students to fill in surrounding circles with information regarding the word. Figure 4.4 shows a simple word map for the word *integer*.

This format can be infinitely modified to help students dig out subtle facets of word meanings by altering the categories related to the word. Consider how the following prompts might help students explore concepts such as *philanthropy, capitalism,* or *radioactivity.*

- What is it like?
- Who would use this word? Who would be unlikely to use this word?
- What other words have the same prefix, suffix, or root?

Figure 4.3. Word Connection Log

New Word	Definition *(explanation of the word that makes sense to you)*	Connection *(example, illustration, association with another word or idea)*
clone	An identical copy of something	Dolly, the sheep, was the first mammal ever cloned from an adult cell.

FIGURE 4.4. Sample Word Map for Mathematical Term

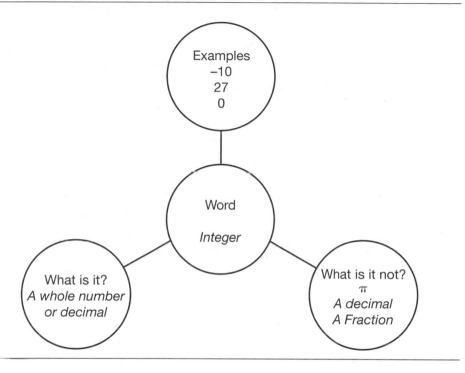

- What does it do?
- How, when, why, and where does it happen?
- What does it smell, feel, taste, sound, or look like?
- What are its benefits?
- What are its costs or problems?
- What types exist?
- What is its connotation?
- What are its synonyms? Its antonyms?
- What are its stages?
- What are arguments for it? Against it?
- How would it be illustrated?

Categorizing Words

An effective activity to help students broaden their understanding of a concept is listing, grouping, and labeling words related to the subject, especially once students have been introduced to the topic (Taba, 1967). For example, if the topic is the Vietnam War, have students brainstorm words or phrases related to the topic, such as *rice paddies, Saigon, Vietcong, tunnel rats, guerrilla warfare, protesters, Lyndon Johnson, Robert McNamara, camouflage, Napalm, Agent Orange, jungle,* and *Vietnam Memorial*. They will then group related words by noting similarities or differences. Finally, students will label each group of related words. If students work in groups, they may label each list differently and explain their thinking, thus providing multiple and varied exposures to words. A labeling of words related to the Vietnam War might look like the example in Figure 4.5.

William Nagy contends that the three properties necessary for powerful vocabulary instruction are integration, repetition, and meaningful use (Nagy, 2004). The above practice can be extended to provide rich vocabulary instruction by integrating, repeating, and using these words as students compare the Vietnam War to the Iraq War. They can also read Internet articles or view news reports from each war to provide a wider context for the words they are learning while stimulating engagement and building background knowledge.

Clarifying Words

A semantic feature analysis (Johnson & Pearson, 1984), much like a Venn diagram, is a tool that helps students analyze and clarify words by exploring their relationships and determining common characteristics. For example, while studying types of simple invertebrates in 10th-grade biology, students could create a semantic feature analysis similar to the one in Figure 4.6. The challenge increases if students determine the categories for each invertebrate or add explanations that expand the categories. After an initial introduction to the vocabulary, students can elaborate on their understandings by reading articles online—for instance, about how parasitic worms affect the health of populations in underdeveloped parts of the world.

FIGURE 4.5. Listing and Labeling of Words Related to the Vietnam War

People	Places	Tools of War
Lyndon Johnson	Rice paddies	Guerrilla tactics
Robert McNamara	Vietnam Memorial	camouflage
Tunnel rats	jungle	Napalm
Viet Cong	Saigon	Agent Orange

FIGURE 4.6. Semantic Feature Analysis of Simple Invertebrates

Simple Invertebrate	Symmetrical	Parasitic	Sexual Repro- duction	Assexual Repro- duction	Aquatic Environ- ment
Sponge			+	+	+
Cnidarian	+ (radially symmetrical)		+	+	+
Flatworm	+ (bilaterally symmetrical)	+	+	+	+ (and moist habitats on land)
Roundworm	+ (bilaterally symmetrical)	+ (and free- living)	+		+ (as well as soil and animals)

Thinking about Words

Nagy (2004) estimates that from 25 to 50% of annual vocabulary growth can be attributed to incidental learning from context while reading; however, many students simply skim over words they don't know without using clues embedded in the context to help them unlock meaning. The guide below will help students become conscious of words they don't know as they are reading and then make a conscious decision about how (or to what extent) they should learn them.

If you encounter an unfamiliar word, ask yourself:

Do I need to know the meaning of this word in order to comprehend the passage?

- Is it in bold print or repeated within the text?
- Is it a word I've heard before in other contexts?

If you don't think you need to know the word:

- Skip the word and continue reading, perhaps noting it in your word log.

If you think you need to know the word, ask yourself:

- Does it remind me of any other word(s) that I know?
  Look at word parts—prefixes, suffixes, roots.
  Does it sound like a word I've heard before?
- Does reading the sentence again provide any additional clues?
- Are there any visual clues, such as illustrations or graphs, to help me understand the word?
- What do I think the word might mean? What makes sense?
- Would a classmate know the meaning? Is the teacher available to explain the meaning?
- Is there a glossary, dictionary, or hypertext that might provide a definition or explain the word?

Although such a thorough analysis of each unfamiliar word may seem cumbersome at first, the goal is to have students internalize the process to become independent in their word study.

WORD STUDY AFTER READING

Marzano cites an essential characteristic of effective vocabulary instruction as one that involves "the gradual shaping of word meanings through multiple exposures" (Marzano, 2004, p. 73). This "shaping" should continue after reading to reinforce and expand content vocabulary. Students conceptualize words more deeply by discussing, defending, and deciding what they believe about words as well as by using them in various contexts. Following are examples of activities that help students reinforce word meanings.

- Provide questions that will allow students to engage in a discussion about a word in various contexts as they consider shades of meaning. Consider the following questions about the word *loyalty*, which might come up in a history class when studying the Civil War or in an English class when reading *Fallen Angels* (Myers, 1988).

  How far should loyalty extend?

  If someone you love breaks the law, under what circumstances is it disloyal to report him or her to the police?

> Does a parent's loyalty to a child differ from a coach's loyalty to a player? If so, how?
>
> Is it disloyal to disagree with the government about actions it takes, such as going to war?

- Show videos that provide opportunities for students to broaden their conceptual understanding of the words, such as having high school students watch parts of *The Last King of Scotland* (2006) as they examine facets of the word *loyalty*.

Middle school students could engage in the same type of dialogue after reading the young adult novel *Crossing Jordan* (Fogelin, 2002) in English.

- Have students engage in a panel discussion or debate about vocabulary that encourages different perspectives, such as the term *stem cell research* or *eminent domain*.
- Have students research a term online, such as *recidivism*, then return to the word maps they created earlier and add other categories to show their increased understanding.
- Designate a bulletin board for political cartoons, comic strips, quotes, music lyrics, and words cut from magazines or newspapers related to the topic of study.
- Provide independent reading time with books or magazines related to the subject to reinforce vocabulary. Reading aloud to students from a relevant book or article, if only for 5 to 10 minutes a day, will significantly improve students' vocabulary. Several young adult novels use vocabulary words in nontraditional ways, such as *The Lightning Thief* (Riordan, 2006) or *When My Name Was Keoko* (Parks, 2004) for middle school students and *A Northern Light* (Donnelly, 2004) or *You Don't Know Me* (Klass, 2002) for high school students.
- Create a carousel activity where small groups of students go from chart to chart discussing words that are related to a unit of study. For example, if students are studying the parts of a cell, write the word that describes each cell part on a separate sheet of chart paper and place the charts on the walls around the room. The small groups will move from chart to chart, writing what they know about the word or phrase. Use the completed charts as a review, asking specific groups why they chose certain words or phrases to describe cell parts.

INTEGRATING CONCEPTS

Word study is an ongoing part of content study, building upon itself as students' knowledge increases. The more opportunities students have to become exposed to words through reading and to use new words through writing, vocabulary activities, and discussion, the more their content knowledge will deepen. Effective and habitual vocabulary instruction is essential for increasing understanding of concepts, building background for future learning, and sharpening skills that are necessary for comprehension.

Principles for Vocabulary Study

- Determine which words are most important for academic study.
- Help students build on their existing knowledge of words.
- Involve students in activities that broaden conceptual understanding of words.
- Spend time on vocabulary instruction before, during, and after reading.
- Include multiple and varied exposures to words through contextual activities.
- Provide collaborative word study activities.
- Show students how to become conscious of words in their reading and make choices about how they will learn new words.

Quote for Reflection

"Words mean more than what is set down on paper.
It takes the human voice to infuse them with deeper meaning."

—Maya Angelou

Study Group Resources

Allen, J. (2007). *Inside words: Tools for teaching academic vocabulary: Grades 4–12.* Portland, ME: Stenhouse.

Beck, I. L., McKeown, M. G., & Kucan, L. (2002). *Bringing words to life: Robust vocabulary instruction.* New York: Guilford.

Graves, M. (2006). *The vocabulary book: Learning & instruction.* New York: Teachers College Press.

Nagy, W. (1988). *Teaching vocabulary to improve reading comprehension.* Newark, DE: International Reading Association.

CHAPTER 5

Reading for Deep Understanding

W E OFTEN HEAR ABOUT HOW THE testing culture has seriously undercut deep and thoughtful reading. Teachers report feeling the uncomfortable "rock and hard place" environment that forces them to choose between "teaching to the test" and taking the necessary time to help students learn in meaningful ways. Pair that dilemma with their near panic over covering all of the topics in the curriculum, and what we have is, as Linda Darling-Hammond put it, "a mentioning curriculum" (Darling-Hammond, 2008).

SUPERFICIAL COVERAGE VERSUS DEEP STUDY

A ninth-grade science teacher recently described his students as being "lost" while he zoomed through topics at breakneck speed in an impossible race to cover units that someone, somewhere, deemed important. When I asked him why he didn't just slow down and cover the most critical topics in depth, allowing students to explore concepts that might spark lifelong learning, he said he didn't feel that was an option. He was convinced that being a good science teacher meant "teaching" his students virtually every topic listed in their textbook's table of contents. I made the argument that although he was teaching his heart out, the students were learning only enough to pass a test, by his own account. He shook his head sadly, not persuaded that he could change his practice.

This unfortunate paradox is all too common in content-area classes: Good teachers who care about their students feel the weight of a mandate to "cover" the textbook, as if this one book created the curriculum instead of being a resource to support it. It is hard to change such beliefs and practices, even in the face of core learning principles identified in respected studies such as the National Research Council's *How People Learn: Brain, Mind, Experience, and School* (2000), which states clearly that "Superficial coverage of all topics in a subject area must be replaced with in-depth coverage of fewer topics that allow key concepts in that discipline to be understood" (p. 20). When I was making this point at a workshop, an anatomy teacher explained how her students explored a topic in depth when a guest speaker described his rather serious knee injury. They spent a week diagnosing his condition and recommending treatment based on their reading from medical journals and the textbook, as well as through interviews with medical professionals. The students presented their findings to the speaker, who revealed the condition and treatment (Lent, 2007). The teacher supported my argument by emphatically stating that her students' knowledge of anatomy soared when students were allowed the time to internalize and transfer their learning.

REDEFINING READING

In the context of such active, engaged learning, the perception of reading will change from a "boring" assigned activity, as in "Read the next chapter," to a useful vehicle for gaining knowledge. Consider the definition of reading offered in a position statement by the National Council of Teachers of English: "Reading is a complex and purposeful sociocultural, cognitive, and linguistic process in which readers simultaneously use their knowledge of spoken and written language, their knowledge of the topic of the text, and their knowledge of their culture to construct meaning with text." This comprehensive definition describes what I call *profound* reading. It eschews the idea that when students correctly pronounce words or accurately interpret diagrams, they are reading in meaningful ways. Reading is, indeed, complex and requires skills that can't be easily measured, but it is a process that becomes joyfully obvious when we see students working through subtle layers of text that may denote different meanings to different readers. Plumbing such depth requires explicit coaching on the part of the teacher, a safe intellectual environment that rewards inquiry, and a good dose of time and patience.

A word about reading strategies. Unfortunately, strategies are sometimes used as creative worksheets with all students "filling in the blanks" at the same time. Often, entire schools choose a "Strategy of the Week." While this practice may help students become familiar with the types of strategies that are available, such practices are not elixirs that will transform disinterested students into critical readers. The goal is for students themselves to become independent, *strategic* readers, appropriately choosing strategies that work best for them. As David Pearson told an audience at a Florida reading conference, "The trick with strategies, ultimately, is knowing which ones will help you in which situations" (Pearson, 2008).

COMPREHENSION MONITORING AND METACOGNITION

Students sometimes read the way they dream—in an unconscious state where events represented by words or visuals move around in their heads in a hazy, ill-defined pattern. They may not even be aware that they are dream-reading. When this happens, students must learn how to set an internal "wake-up" alarm. Even then, they may not know how to alter their reading so that the *way* they read reflects their purpose, the text itself, or their intrinsic interest in the topic.

Helping students recognize their own reading behaviors is a critical step toward independent learning. Comprehension monitoring, according to a report titled *Adolescents and Literacy: Reading for the 21st Century* (2004) by Michael Kamil, is "the process by which readers decide whether or not they are understanding the text" (p. 13).

In the context of reading, metacognition refers to readers' abilities to predict and monitor their performances on tasks as well as their understanding. Teaching practices that utilize a metacognitive approach include those that focus on "sense-making, self-assessment, and reflection on what worked and what needs improving" (National Research Council, 2002, p. 12). Several studies have demonstrated that when metacognitive strategies are incorporated into topics of study, understanding in subjects such as physics, writing, and mathematical problem solving increases (National Research Council, 2002).

You can help students become reflective about their own reading and learning by asking them to complete a survey such as the one in Figure 5.1. Consider offering students a particularly difficult text, such as a passage from a book written in your subject area before 1900, to help them "observe" their reading behaviors. You may also want to read aloud a text that is challenging and explain to students how you, as a proficient reader, monitor your own comprehension to let you know if and when you're "getting it." Texts from different disciplines work well, too, such as a math teacher reading a difficult piece of poetry or an English teacher reading a complex word problem. Official documents such as income tax instructions or insurance policies also can be used to demonstrate how anyone, even teachers with college degrees, can struggle with text. When you come to a phrase that is difficult to understand, talk through your mental process of comprehension by rereading, asking questions about what the author might mean, or focusing on a word that is hard to understand. In keeping with the theme of this book, for example, consider how I might explain my thinking as I read aloud the following passage from an article in *Newsweek* titled "The Future of Reading" (Levy, 2007).

Text: Long before there was cyberspace, books led us to a magical nether-zone.

Me: I haven't heard the word *nether-zone* before; I wonder if the author made it up. I know *nether* means "under," like

FIGURE 5.1. Metacognition Survey

Think about your behaviors as a reader. Then, finish each sentence.

When reading, I become more easily distracted if . . .

It is easier for me to become distracted when reading _____ than when reading _____.

I can focus when I am reading . . .

The subject that I have the most difficult reading is _____ because . . .

When reading to answer questions, I . . .

When reading to remember something, I . . .

When reading for enjoyment, I . . .

I comprehend best when . . .

The type of text that I read with the most understanding is _____ because _____. (Consider all types of text, not just what you read for school, when answering the above question.)

One of the things I do to help myself stay focused is . . .

When I come to a vocabulary word I don't know, I . . .

When text becomes confusing or difficult, I . . .

I remember important points in the text by . . .

I understand information presented in a chart or diagram by . . .

I find meaning in a photograph by . . .

It is easier for me to read _____ than _____ because . . .

It is more difficult for me to read _____ than _____ because . . .

When I read something with which I disagree, I . . .

I read online articles differently than print-based articles in the following ways:

"underworld" in mythology, and the word *magical* preceding it seems to support that idea.

Text: "Books are all the dreams we would most like to have and like dreams they have the power to change consciousness," wrote Victor Nell in a 1988 tome called *Lost in a Book*.

Me: I don't know Victor Nell, but his book sounds like one I would like. It's interesting that I wrote about readers as dreamers, but I didn't think about dreams changing consciousness.

Text: Nell coined a name for that trance-like state that heavy readers enter when consuming books for pleasure—"ludic reading"(from the Latin *ludo*, meaning "I play.") Annie Proulx's claim was that an electronic device would never create that hypnotic state. But technologists are disproving that.

Me: If the author hadn't told me about the Latin root, I wouldn't have had a clue about the meaning of *ludic*. Annie Proulx wrote *Shipping News*, a book I like, but why did the author quote her? I will keep reading to find out how technologists are disproving her statement, because I tend to agree with her.

Take time to engage students in a dialogue about how they can help themselves become better readers of text in your content area. For instance, ask them what historians do when they read (interpret documents, apply principles from one historical event to another, read skeptically) or what scientists do (understand vocabulary as it relates to science, utilize the scientific process, analyze data). List their responses on a chart, add to it yourself, and post it as a reminder of the habits of proficient readers in your domain. A troubleshooting chart like the one in Figure 5.2 may also encourage students to stop reading when they are having difficulties and take action to get back on track.

RECIPROCAL TEACHING

An effective way to help students develop metacognition is an activity called reciprocal teaching (Palincsar & Brown, 1986). As the name implies, this practice allows students to learn as they teach and, as we all know, teaching is one of the best ways to come to know a subject well. Reciprocal teaching is based on dialogue among students as well as between teachers and students. The dialogue is structured through summarizing, question generating, clarifying, and predicting. A traditional reciprocal teaching session might look something like this:

- The teacher reads a key passage or shows students a photograph, primary document, graph, or chart, and then summarizes the content.
- The teacher asks students questions about the text as well as questions that require students to think critically.
- The teacher clarifies any difficult concepts, vocabulary, language, or misconceptions.
- The students predict what will come next in the text.
- Students practice the skills in small groups.

Student Study Groups

In secondary classes, an engaging way to utilize reciprocal teaching is to have students form student study groups and take roles that focus on each of the above skills. Much like the literature circles that English teachers use to help students delve into the underlying meanings of short stories, novels, and poems, this practice encourages students to focus the discussion as they help one another comprehend content-area text. For a more complete description of literature circles, go to www.literaturecircles.com.

Willard Brown, a science teacher at Skyline High School in Oakland, California, wrote about his students' experiences with what he terms "Team-Reads," a form of reciprocal teaching where students alternate between "reading a small amount of text individually while making notes about their reading and thinking processes and then discussing the section with three teammates" (Greenleaf, Brown, & Litman, 2004, p. 217). He provides role cards to facilitate discussion with reading strategy reminders, as well as discussion prompts to keep the dialogue going. Roles include the following:

- *Clarifier*—Helps team members find clear purpose of the text
    - Sample Reading Strategy Reminder (SRSR): "Look for the author's ideas, hypotheses, and evidence."
    - Sample Discussion Prompt (SDP): "What can we do to understand this?"

Figure 5.2. Reading Trouble-Shooting Chart

The Challenge	The Reading Lifeline
You almost "get" it, but not quite.	Reread.
You "get" the overall idea, but the details escape you.	Discuss what you are reading with someone else, clarifying points that support the "big picture."
You don't understand much of what you are reading or viewing.	• Ask someone who understands the content to explain it to you and then reread. • Look up the topic online to build background knowledge.
You can recite facts from the text, but you really don't understand what the author is trying to communicate.	• Go back and/or read ahead, looking at nonprint features of the text (graphs, charts, illustrations, chapter titles, words in bold). • Try to identify important parts of the text and skim through those passages again. • Read through the table of contents, the introduction, or the text on the back of the book. • Think of questions you would like to ask the author and continue reading to see if your questions have been answered.
You are having trouble understanding because you don't know enough about the subject to "put it all together."	Build your background knowledge by finding information from another text on the same topic, such as an online resource, a book, magazine, video, or by talking to someone who is knowledgeable about the subject.
You feel as if you are reading a foreign language.	Determine key vocabulary you don't know and find the meaning by using context clues, asking someone for meanings, or using a dictionary or glossary.
You find yourself distracted or bored when you read, and are unable to concentrate.	• Read more quickly or slow down, forcing yourself to pay attention by stopping at intervals to think (or talk about) what you have read. • Take mental or physical breaks from the text. • Try to visualize what is happening, placing yourself within the text rather than reading as an observer. • Set a purpose for reading, even a small one to keep you focused.

The Challenge	The Reading Lifeline
You understand what you are reading up to a certain point and then you seem to lose it.	• Summarize what you have read so far, either by talking to someone, reviewing it out loud, or writing about it. • Try to predict what might come next. Read to find out if your predictions are correct. • Try to pinpoint when the confusion started and go back and reread a few paragraphs before that point.
You have difficulty because you disagree with the author or have strong feelings about the text.	• Write to explore your feelings about the text and gain understanding of the author's viewpoint. • Return to the text and mentally engage the author in a conversation or debate about the issues. Think about what you would say to the author to change his or her mind. • Remember that you have the right to your opinion about a text. Allow yourself time to stop and think through what is bothering you.
You've reread but you still don't get it.	• Read the text orally or ask someone to read it to you. • Try to pinpoint what is confusing and ask your teacher or someone else to help you clarify.
You are having trouble knowing what is important in the text.	• Set a purpose for reading. Tell yourself that you will read a part of the text for a specific reason (such as to find out why something happened) and concentrate only on that purpose. • Use a double-column note-taking approach, "What's Important" on one side and "Why?" or "What's Interesting?" on the other. • If you are reading a textbook, look at chapter headings, words in bold, and captions for illustrations or charts.

• *Questioner*—Helps team members ask and answer questions about the text

   SRSR: "What evidence supports the author's ideas?"
   SDP: "Which questions did you have or wonder about as you read?"

- *Summarizer*—Helps the team members restate the main ideas and key facts in their own words

    SRSR: "Summaries are formed by the reader, not stated in the text."

    SDP: "How can we combine ideas into one summary?"

- *Predictor*—Helps the team connect sections of the text by reviewing predictions from the previous sections and asking them to use clues to predict what they will read next

    SRSR: "Predictions help us check our understanding and keep us engaged."

    SDP: "Were any of our predictions about the section we just read correct?" (Greenleaf, Brown, & Litman, 2004, p. 217)

Expanding Roles

You can adapt the above activity by writing questions on the board that are specific to your content to facilitate discussion. You may also want to experiment with various roles that address topics students are studying, such as the following example for a text on genetics in science.

- The role of summarizer is a DNA/RNA resource person who will summarize the function of DNA and RNA in genetics.
- The role of clarifier is an illustrator who will clarify the concepts through drawings, charts, comic strips, or other visual aids.
- The predictor will focus on how vocabulary will be used in future reading. For example, the vocabulary predictor may explain "-tion" words such as *mutation*, *replication*, and *transcription* and then lead the group to make predictions about how such key vocabulary might be used in the next chapter, passage, or video.
- The question-generator in this case will assume the role of a writer who is finding information for an article about various genetic disorders. The group will help her create questions she needs answered in order to write the article.

As you can see, there is no end to the way roles can be varied to explore meaning in text. Teachers who use this approach report that students are highly engaged in the process, as it allows for social interaction and collaboration, important practices that facilitate deep reading.

INTEGRATING CONCEPTS

Reading for deep understanding requires awareness—about the text, the author's meaning, and, perhaps most important, about oneself as a reader. Such awareness is not enough, however. The reader must become a participant in the process, talking with others about the ideas presented by the author, asking questions while reading, and taking the time to implement meaning in all its forms.

Principles for Deep Understanding

- Cover fewer topics in more depth by providing a variety of texts and project-based inquiry projects.
- Show students what it means to read strategically by teaching them to monitor their comprehension.
- Allow students to explore texts collaboratively by using reciprocal teaching activities that promote independent learning.

Quote for Reflection

"The ability to read awoke inside me some long dormant craving to be mentally alive."

—Malcolm X

Study Group Resources

Beers, K., Probst, R. E., & Rief, L. (Eds.). (2007). *Adolescent literacy: Turning promise into practice.* Portsmouth, NH: Heinemann.

Daniels, H., & Zemelman, S. (2004). *Every teacher's guide to content-area reading.* Portsmouth, NH: Heinemann.

Lewis, J., & Moorman, G. (Eds.). (2007). *Adolescent literacy instruction: Policy and promising practices.* Newark, DE: International Reading Association.

National Research Council. (2000). *How people learn: Brain, mind, experience, and school* (2nd ed.). Washington, DC: National Academy Press.

CHAPTER 6

Reading and Thinking Critically

WHEN I ASKED A GROUP OF ninth-grade students if they believed that everything written in their textbooks was true, they looked from me to their teacher as if I were in danger of being suspended. Not one student responded. "Who do you think writes textbooks?" I asked. The ensuing dialogue left no doubt that these students believe that text generally, and textbooks in particular, are like sacred documents written by infallible, omniscient beings. Many students do not question the accuracy or objectivity of information presented in textbooks, handouts, articles in magazines, or information they access online. For the most part, if students doubt the veracity of what they read, they keep it to themselves. In fact, many students report to me that they don't care if what they are reading is true, as long as they pass the class. This mentality is in sharp contrast to classrooms where active engagement is an inherent part of students' reading and learning process, where they are encouraged to look not only at what is being presented but also at how it is presented, by whom, and why.

CRITICAL LITERACY

Ron Ritchhart describes critical thinkers as those who open-mindedly evaluate information, maintain a healthy skepticism until all the facts are in, and attempt to hold their bias in check as they consider evidence. They use logic to solve problems by clarifying, considering the viability of alternative solutions, and setting steps to resolve the problem (Ritchhart, 2004). Critical literacy taps into a similar process and includes "understanding the ways in which language and literacy are used to accomplish social ends" (Dozier, Johnston, & Rogers, 2006, p. 18). More than a set of skills, critical literacy requires "understanding literacy as a tool for social action and understanding the ways in which that tool works" (p. 19). Critical readers in any content area, according to the author of an article that examines practices supporting critical literacy, must pay attention to the "interrelationships of language, power, and text" (Behrman, 2006, p. 497). In other words, students must understand that texts have multiple meanings with varying perspectives based on an author's intent and motives.

Addressing Critical Literacy through Habits of Mind

As teachers help students become proficient *and* critical readers, they often utilize thinking dispositions or habits of mind. Art Costa and Bena Kallick describe 16 behaviors in their book series *Habits of Mind: A Developmental Series* (2000). A policy document titled *Project 2061: Science for All Americans* lists seven habits of mind, including integrity, diligence, fairness, curiosity, openness to new ideas, skepticism, and imagination. Some schools develop or adapt their own habits of mind, such as Central Park East Secondary School, whose "habits" have "worked well to guide instruction and have withstood the test of time at that school" (Ritchhart, 2004, p. 26). As an example, Central Park's five habits of mind include the following:

Evidence: How do we know?
Viewpoint: Who is speaking?
Connections: What causes this?
Supposition: How might things be different?
Meaningfulness: What's the point? Why does it matter?

Using the above questions, consider how middle or high school students in an English or social studies class might critically investigate the civil rights movement as well as specific events related to it, such as the horrific murder of Emmett Till in 1955, by using the above questions. Be aware that dialogue such as the following may create some discomfort as students examine difficult issues. Such cognitive dissonance, however, is a positive step in thinking critically, especially if students have learned to respect divergent opinions.

- Evidence: How do we know the events surrounding Emmett Till's murder are true?

    What sources have we used to gain information?
    How do we know the sources are accurate?
    How does the information in one source compare to information in another source?

- Viewpoint: Who is speaking about the murder?

    Who is speaking when you read each primary document regarding Till's murder?
    Who was speaking when the murder was committed?
    Who is speaking in the book *Death of Innocence: The Story of the Hate Crime That Changed America* by Mamie Till-Mobley and Christopher Benson (2004)?
    Who is speaking in the PBS Documentary *American Experience—The Murder of Emmett Till* (2003)?

- Connections: What caused the murder of Emmett Till?

    What are the underlying causes of crimes such as these?
    What causes people to hate others they don't know?
    What causes discrimination to continue to be a problem in America and other parts of the world?

- Supposition: How might things have been different?

    What, if anything, could Emmett Till's uncle have done to prevent his murder?

What, if anything, could society have done to prevent
the murder?
How could laws have prevented the murder?

- Meaningfulness: What's the point? Why does it matter?

    Why does this particular murder have more
    significance than others?
    Why does it matter that Emmett Till is remembered?
    How did this crime change the thinking of people
    during the civil rights movement? Today?

The transformative power of critical reading and thinking is evident as the text morphs from an abstract, objective line of "facts"
into meaning that remains with students long after the lesson has
ended. Habits of mind also teach more than content—they help
students respond to an author's ideas in relation to who they are
rather than as passive observers accepting everything they read or
view at face value. Students who begin to assume responsibility
for their own understanding and learn how to engage in generative dialogue are taking the first steps toward creating societal and
cultural change.

Addressing Critical Literacy by Questioning the Author

An effective activity for helping students read critically is *Improving Comprehension with Questioning the Author* (Beck & McKeown,
2006). When students question the author, they evaluate information
presented by the author as well as his or her motivation for writing. They may question why an author includes or excludes specific
information or what the writer means by certain words, phrases, or
passages. For example, when reading an article from *Newsweek* titled
"Teens, Tans, and Truth" (Wingert, 2008), students who visit tanning
beds may want to know the following before changing their tanning
habits:

- Who wrote the article?
- Is the writer biased toward one position or another?
- How reliable is *Newsweek* as a source?
- Why did the author include information from the Indoor
  Tanning Association?
- Why did the author include information from the
  American Cancer Society?

- Why did the author include quotes from students who frequent tanning beds?
- In what way do tanning beds represent teens' values?
- What important information might be missing from the article?
- What other visuals might have been included to make the article more interesting or understandable?
- Do you feel the author is successful in making her point?
- If you wrote a letter to the editor, how would you respond to this article?
- If this were an online article, what hypertexts might be included?

ACTIVITIES THAT FOSTER CRITICAL THINKING AND READING

Following are other suggestions for helping students learn to read and think critically.

- Have students read a common text from various points of view, especially one that is based on true events. For example, high school students may read *The Translator: A Tribesman's Memoir of Darfur* (Hari, 2008), and discuss Darfur's tragedy from the point of view of the author, a member of his family, journalists from around the world, and the American government. Use the same type of activity with middle school students when they read *Tree Girl* (Mikaelsen, 2004), a young adult novel based on a true story about the massacres in Guatemala in 1980.
- Help students learn to evaluate commercials or advertisements and discuss how companies use methods of persuasion to sell their products. See *Hey, Kidz! Buy This Book: A Radical Primer on Corporate and Governmental Propaganda and Artistic Activism for Short People* (Moore, 2004) to jump-start the discussion.
- Teach students how to identify common propaganda techniques when assessing visual and print-based text. You may want to download a lesson from Read-Write-Think that shows students how to identify propaganda techniques used in literature and online political cartoons: http://www.readwritethink.org/lessons/lesson_view. asp?id=405. The site also has several links directly

relevant to content-area study, such as an examination of propaganda used during the Cold War.

- Give students a current events topic, such as the U.S. immigration debate, and have them analyze the coverage from different sources, such as Fox, CNN, and National Public Radio. Place students in three different groups to listen to, read, or view their assigned news piece and then provide a summary to the class, focusing on words that might be coercive or "loaded." The class will decide which source is most objective by comparing reports.

- Provide students with song lyrics that contain a political message such as "The Hand That Feeds" by Nine Inch Nails, a criticism of the Iraq war, or even John Lennon's "Imagine." Provocative documentaries also work well for this activity, such as *Brother Outsider: The Life of Bayard Rustin* (2003), the narrative of a civil rights activist who worked behind the scenes because he feared his homosexuality would have a negative influence on the movement. Have students explore such texts from perspectives that include race, gender, class, ethnicity, or sexuality.

- Provide students with multiple texts on the same topic, such as the example from Chapter 1 that encourages using a variety of texts related to the Holocaust. "Students can consider who constructed the text, when, where, why, and the values on which it was based. By experiencing different treatments of the same topic or event, students begin to recognize that text is not 'true' in any absolute sense but a rendering as portrayed by an author" (Behrman, 2006, p. 492).

ASSESSING CRITICAL READING AND THINKING

If traditional testing does not assess critical thinking skills, then how should teachers assess such student learning? Consider alternative assessments that give "teachers and students a more complete picture of student progress than do traditional assessments such as multiple choice, short answer, essay and standardized tests" (Lewis & Moorman, 2007, p. 152). Alternatives may include electronic or paper portfolios, videos of students working together, inquiry-based projects and presentations, checklists of behaviors, student-teacher conferences, and relevant, purposeful writing. Wiggins and McTighe (1998) have examined deep learning through their *Learning by Design* materials, including a book by the same name. In it, they present a view of what makes up "mature understanding." You may want to use their facets of understanding to develop reading assignments or to assess students' levels of understanding:

- Can students explain learning through supported and justifiable accounts of phenomena, facts, and data?
- Can students apply what they have learned in diverse contexts?
- Have students developed perspective so they can critically see and hear points of view and see the big picture?
- Can students empathize and find value in what others might find odd or implausible?
- Have students acquired self-knowledge to perceive what shapes and impedes our own understanding? (p. 44)

CHALLENGING TEXTS

As students become adept at reading critically, they must be provided with texts that are challenging enough to stimulate their thinking. Unfortunately, many traditional secondary texts do not provide such stimulation. In their book *Reading Don't Fix No Chevys*, Michael Smith and Jeff Wilhelm quote secondary students who overwhelmingly found their schoolwork to be insufficiently challenging. One student described the work he was asked to do in many classes as "mind numbing." The authors point out that this same boy was reading a complex psychological study of the roots of evil on his own (Smith & Wilhelm, 2002, p. 114). Ask students what they read or view out of school on a daily basis, and you will find that, in many ways, today's teens are voracious and sophisticated readers. Students all over the country in grades 7–12, for example, are reading the *Twilight* series by Stephanie Meyer. Her books are long by anyone's standard, yet students count down the minutes until her next book is on the shelves. I visited a high school where students had their names on a waiting list to check out the issue of *Time* magazine that contained an article about the author: "Stephanie Meyer: A New J. K. Rowling" (Grossman, 2008).

Unfortunately, many students are denied opportunities to read engaging, stimulating text because, once again, high-stakes standardized tests interfere. The results of such tests often inaccurately mark students with a single, dismissive label: remedial, struggling, or at risk—tags that forecast their placement in intensive reading classes or their absence from interesting, often challenging, elective courses. Such stereotypes sometimes convince teachers or administrators that these students cannot read complex texts. The learners who most need to be immersed in stimulating reading then fall further behind or may even drop out.

"Students need high-interest and challenging reading material, with models, practice material, and longer selections drawn from sources that are commonly found in academic text," according to Jill Lewis in a book on content-area literacy. She goes on to point out the importance of teaching students to read challenging material. "The ability to read complex tests is the clearest differentiator between students who are more likely to be ready for college-level reading and those who are less likely to be ready" (Lewis & Moorman, 2007, p. 149).

How to Make Challenging Texts Accessible

The concept of offering students challenging texts is also addressed in *Preparing Teachers for a Changing World* (Darling-Hammond & Bransford, 2005). The authors of a chapter titled "Enhancing the Development of Students' Language(s)" contend that students will be able to comprehend such texts as *The Federalist Papers* or *The Autobiography of Frederick Douglass* if they have a "rich understanding of the content on which the text is based and a long personal history of reading such documents" (Valdes, Bunch, Snow, Lee, & Matos, 2005, p. 151). After studying *The Crucible* (Miller, 1996) in high school English or the Salem witch trials in history, for example, students may read *Witch Child* (Rees, 2002), a novel written from the perspective of a 14-year-old girl who believes she may be a witch and leaves England for the "safety" of early America. After students read Rees's book, give them a primary document that challenges them to use a variety of reading and critical thinking skills.

On the U.S. Library of Congress's website, American Memory (http://memory.loc.gov/), you will find an extensive collection of historical documents and artifacts, more than 7 million items, in fact. A search for "Salem witch trials" locates primary documents that include a "Witches' Petition" from 1692, an appeal from ten women who were confined without trial in a jail for many months. The document begins, "The humble petition of us whose names are subscribed hereonto now prisoners at Ipswich. . . ." Although this petition is difficult to comprehend, especially since it contains unfamiliar spellings such as "weake and infirme," students will persist in finding meaning in the unfamiliar language as they read about the women pleading to be released on "bayle" so they do not "perish with cold" during the winter months. This document, combined with *Witch Child*, will lead students to think critically about this unfortunate time in history and ways in which fear has led to the persecution of other groups of people in America's history. Further, the sense of awe that students often feel when they successfully translate such authentic texts often sparks the intrinsic motivation to explore other documents related to the topic.

Challenging Read-Alouds

Read interesting and challenging texts aloud to students, if only a few pages a day, and pepper your reading with thoughtful questions for them to consider. Richard Preston's *Demon in the Freezer* (2003), for example, taught me more about the functions of cells, especially as they respond to the dreaded smallpox, than I ever learned in a science textbook. This book will immerse students in scientific writing that may be too challenging for them to read independently, yet they can become acquainted with specialized vocabulary and essential subject-area concepts while listening to a spellbinding account. Similarly, *Mayflower: The Story of Courage, Community, and War* (Philbrick, 2007) examines the history of the Plymouth Colony in an eye-opening narrative that will enrich students' understanding of this time period while exposing them to exemplary writing. Help students sift through the many facts and assumptions as they learn to read from varying perspectives.

Math teachers have helped students consider problem solving in new ways by reading aloud *The Curious Incident of the Dog in the Night-Time* (Haddon, 2004), a novel written from the point of view of an autistic teenager who thinks mathematically. *London Calling* (Bloor, 2008), a fact-filled novel for English or social studies students about a boy who time-travels to the 1940 Blitz in London, challenges readers as they move from the past to the present with the narrator. *The Astonishing Life of Octavian Nothing: Traitor to the Nation, Volume I: The Pox Party* (Anderson, 2006) provides an even greater level of reading difficulty in a mesmerizing tale that would be appropriate in high school science, social studies, or English classes. The author notes how he used 18th-century diction and grammar and included descriptions of experiments and events that were believed to have occurred at the time. Consider how students could use critical literacy skills as they read the following passage that depicts a discussion between two slaves about their "master" and others like him:

> "This is what they want us to be," he said. "They want us to be nothing but a bill of sale and letter explaining where we is and instructions for where we go and what we do. They want us empty. They want us flat as paper. They want to be able to carry our souls in their hands, and read them out loud in court. All the time, they're on the exploration of themselves, going on the inner journey into their own breast. But us, they want there to be nothing inside of. They want us to be writ on. They want us to be a surface. Look at me; I'm mahogany."
>
> I protested, "A man is known by his deeds."
>
> "Oh that's sure," said Bono. "Just like a house is known by its deeds. The deeds say who owns it, who sold it, and who'll be buying a new one when it gets knocked down." (p. 136)

Many quality books such as the ones recommended above are available on CD as audiobooks, an effective alternative to teacher read-alouds as students can listen to professional readers or actors use inflection, tone, and phrasing effectively to enhance meaning.

Challenging Texts and Self-Efficacy

Providing texts such as those mentioned above does more than build critical readers; it also supports students' self-efficacy, an important component of engagement, as students grapple with complex ideas and eventually learn to make meaning of texts that may seem inaccessible at first glance. Alvermann notes, "It is evident that students with a high *self-efficacy*—the confidence that they have the capacity to produce a desired effect—are more likely to engage in school-related reading than students with low self-efficacy. Perceptions of self-efficacy are central to most theories of motivation, and the research bears out the hypothesized connections" (Alvermann, 2003, p. 2). Teachers play a significant role in helping students gain the self-efficacy they need by offering them challenging materials that establish high expectations for their success.

Nancy Goodwin, retired English teacher, described what many teachers understand intuitively: "So many times, students have never been given the opportunity to discover their own intellectual identity, yet that is the greatest gift we as educators can give: to sincerely and convincingly show students their intellectual potential" (Goodwin, 2008).

INTEGRATING CONCEPTS

Students can learn to read more deeply and critically if they are given the time and opportunity to explore texts in authentic ways. Challenging materials, a context and purpose for reading *all* media, and the freedom to ponder and question will not only eliminate need for "test prep," but will also create learners who have gained the intellectual confidence to succeed.

Principles for Reading Critically

- Help students learn to examine texts in light of purpose, language, and intent.
- Use or develop habits of mind to guide students in reading critically and thoughtfully.
- Show students how to question the author to determine his or her viewpoint, possible bias, and meaning.
- Use authentic assessments that accurately assess critical thinking.
- Provide challenging, relevant texts; show students how to approach them; and expect that students can read them.

Quote for Reflection

"The important thing is not to stop questioning."

—Albert Einstein

Study Group Resources

Costa, A. (2001). *Developing minds: A resource book for teaching thinking* (3rd ed.). Alexandria, VA: Association for Supervision and Curriculum Development.

Doizier, C., Johnston, P., & Rogers, R. (2006). *Critical literacy/critical teaching: Tools for preparing responsive teachers.* New York: Teachers College Press.

Lewis, J., & Moorman, G. (Eds.). (2007). *Adolescent literacy instruction: Policies and promising practices.* Newark, DE: International Reading Association.

Ogle, D., Klemp, R., & McBride, B. (2007). *Building literacy in social studies: Strategies for improving comprehension and critical thinking.* Alexandria, VA: Association for Supervision and Curriculum Development.

CHAPTER 7

Online
Reading

LEANNA LANDSMAN, AUTHOR OF THE syndicated column "A+ Advice for Parents," wrote to me recently asking my advice on the following question:

> Our middle school has "page" reading requirements. By a certain date each month students need to have read a certain number of book pages, fiction and nonfiction. My daughter, who is interested in marine biology, asked her teacher if reading web pages would count for her nonfiction and he said no. Am I missing something? Does reading text on paper do more for a student's intellectual development than reading online?

Although I helped her craft a brief answer, there was so much more to say. I probably should have told Leanna to direct the parent *and* teacher to Julie Coiro's article at www.readinonline.org titled "Reading Comprehension on the Internet: Expanding Our Understanding of Reading Comprehension to Encompass New Literacies" for a short course on how online reading challenges students' intellectual development. In a similar article in *Educational Leadership* (2005), Corio states,

> Reading online is a complex process that requires knowledge about how search engines work and how information is organized within Websites—knowledge that many students lack. Internet text also demands higher levels of inferential reasoning and comprehension monitoring strategies that help readers stay on task. Because today's students need to become proficient in using information and communication technologies to succeed both in school and in a knowledge economy, educators will need to consider how to teach and assess online reading. (Coiro, p. 30)

The idea that print-based reading is somehow *real* reading and online reading a poor substitute is obsolete thinking. In fact, the International Reading Association's position statement on *Integrating Literacy and Technology in the Curriculum* (2001) suggests that traditional definitions of reading, writing, and viewing will soon be insufficient. It's not just educators who understand the changing dynamics of reading and learning, either. A report issued by the Partnership for 21st Century Skills found that 86% of voters say they believe that schools can and should incorporate skills for critical thinking and problem solving, computer and technology, and communication and self-direction into their curriculum (Partnership for 21st Century Skills, 2007).

Our students, sometimes referred to as the "Net Generation," were reared with the Internet as an ever-present part of their lives, just as the generation before them was reared with television or the radio. For these kids, the Internet is not a miracle of technology; it simply exists to serve.

While we all agree that the Internet is an essential tool in students' academic and social lives, what concerns us as educators are students' abilities to deal with the complex skills that online reading demands as well as their proficiency in evaluating web sources for accuracy and reliability.

INTERNET VERSUS PRINT-BASED READING

How does reading print compare to online reading? First, reading online is not a linear activity, as is reading print-based text. Instead, students can quickly find themselves overwhelmed with the sheer number of search-hits leading to related links, hypertexts, music, and flashing visual images. As Coiro (2003) points out, "A reader must understand the advantages and disadvantages associated with having ultimate control of the direction in which text progresses and use inferential reasoning skills and context clues to discern one type of hyperlink from another" (p. 3). Coiro argues that comprehension processes are different on the Internet and that students must extend their "use of traditional comprehension skills to new contexts for learning" such as "electronic searching and tele-collaborative inquiry projects" (p. 8). She poses several questions that could well be the focus of a teacher study group in all secondary schools:

- Is the comprehension process different on the Internet?
- If so, what new thought processes are required beyond those needed to comprehend conventional print?
- Are these processes extensions of traditional comprehension skills or do web-based learning environments demand fundamentally different skills? (p. 1)

Reading the Internet

As you help students become proficient readers of content-area texts, how can you guide them in "reading" the Internet so that they don't become hopelessly lost or duped?

A comprehensive book that addresses these issues is *Teaching with the Internet K–12: New Literacies for New Times* (Leu, Leu, & Corio, 2004). The authors identify several skills that are needed for Internet use, many of which have been addressed earlier in this book as skills that are also required for print-based reading.

- Identify important questions.
  Students need to know how to ask the right questions from Internet sources and when the Internet should be used for exploring a particular issue. For example, an eighth-grader involved in a science project to

determine which fertilizer stimulates the greatest
growth in tomato plants might not use the Internet
extensively for her research. When she does, she
should know which questions the Internet will best
answer. She could, for instance, search for information
regarding the composition of commercial fertilizers
or to find out how compost is created and used, but
she would also want to conduct her own experiments
or interview gardeners about their experiences,
either in person or online. Students must also learn to
continually reframe their initial question as they gather
new information.

- Navigate information networks to locate relevant
information.

    The authors warn that students must learn to maintain
    focus on a task and not be distracted by irrelevant
    information. Students should also be able to select the
    appropriate search engine and learn to navigate rapidly
    through webpages to locate what they need. Students
    in a high school social studies or English class who are
    researching the diamond trade—specifically, "conflict"
    or "blood" diamonds—must be savvy web-searchers
    and maintain focus. Under a search for "diamond
    trade," for example, they will find a reputable museum
    site that gives a history of diamonds with a link about
    why and how diamonds were first used for "love and
    betrothal." Students may want to read this article, but
    should understand that although the information is
    interesting, it is not relevant to the topic of study.

    Teachers should also help students learn to
    "use a listserv, email, Instant Messaging, or other
    communication tools to request and obtain information
    from knowledgeable others" (Leu, Leu, & Coiro, 2004,
    p. 23).

- Critically evaluate the usefulness of the information.

    Students should evaluate and think critically about
    every piece of information found on the Internet
    for usefulness and reliability. They should also
    check multiple sources to determine "truthfulness"
    and analyze each site to determine the stance
    the author takes and how this stance shapes the

information. Students working on a project about
Emily Dickinson, for example, might look to the
Emily Dickinson International Society (www.
emilydickinsoninternationalsociety.org) as a viable
starting point. Although this is a reputable site with
scholarly articles, much of the information may not
be useful; one must even be a member to access
journals and bulletins. Some websites about the poet
may look professional but may have been created by
other students or may contain superficial information
or opinions. Students also must learn to compare
websites, such as biographical information on the
Academy of American Poets' site (www.poets.org)
to the ubiquitous Wikipedia to determine which
offers the most accurate information that will fit their
needs. Finally, the authors recommend that teachers
help students "understand the significant of URL
endings in terms of what purposes might be served by
information at a site" (Leu, Leu, & Coiro, 2004, p. 24).

- Synthesize information to answer the question or solve the
problem.

    Students should learn how to bookmark information
    and synthesize multiple sources of information,
    perhaps with the use of digital mapping tools (Leu,
    Leu, & Coiro, 2004, p. 24). Just as students learn to
    use graphic organizers appropriately for print-based
    texts, they will find them helpful when faced with the
    often overwhelming amount of online information. See
    Chapter 3 resources for using graphic organizers.

- Communicate the answer to others.

    Students should know how to use email, Instant
    Messaging, weblogs, webpages, or video conferencing
    technologies for communication purposes. (Leu,
    Leu, & Coiro, 2004, p. 24). Provide tasks for students
    that include using Internet communication tools,
    such as requiring that they have at least one email
    communication with an authority in the field when
    doing a research project. Bring in guest speakers from
    the business community, such as engineers, nurses, or
    editors, to show students how such tools are used in
    work settings.

Adapting Print-Based Reading Skills

Watch students at home as they adeptly scan the web for the information they need: the type of surfboard or snowboard that is best for their ability level and price range, car insurance rates, reviews of videogames. They have learned how to read the web as pros; they know what they want, how to quickly access information, and what to do with it once they have it. The challenge is to help students transfer the skills they already have to academic tasks. This will take explicit instruction and convincing students to slow down enough to become intentional, rather than instinctual, in their digital endeavors.

A social studies and reading teacher in a rural high school collaborated to allow their students to conduct online research for projects about World War I for a school-wide Veteran's Day assembly. One group of students generated a slide show for the beginning of the program and others created informative posters to display on hallway walls as the audience entered the auditorium. Several students gave oral readings and others created handouts to accompany guest speakers' presentations. Because they had a limited amount of time to complete their projects and their labor was to be on display, students had to work efficiently and accurately. The Reading Trouble-Shooting Chart in Chapter 5 reminded them of strategies they could employ if they became "stuck." They also used the guide in Figure 7.1 to make their online research more productive.

READING CRITICALLY ONLINE

As students were conducting online research about World War I, they found an abundance of information. They soon learned, however, to become skeptical readers in evaluating webpages for reliability and accuracy. Most students know that anyone can post anything on the web and that the information is unregulated and unmonitored, but they may not know how to evaluate the truthfulness of sites. Before beginning their projects, show students examples of hoax sites, the most famous being the "Pacific Northwest Tree Octopus" (http://zapatopi.net/treeoctopus/) and demonstrate how seemingly reputable sites with references to well-known sources can be completely false. They may also enjoy perusing

FIGURE 7.1. Online Reading Skills

Reading Skill	Applying the Skill to Online Text
Previewing	Once you access a home page, skim it to preview what it contains. Look at the titles of the links, the source, the vocabulary, and any graphs or photographs. Make an informed decision about whether or not this site is worth your time.
Summarizing	Find important points in an article and write a brief summary to help you keep track of what each site offers. These summaries will be invaluable as you synthesize information into a report. It may be helpful to create a summary form that has the site on the left side and a summary on the right.
Predicting	Predict what information hypertexts or links on the home pages may contain before clicking onto the links. This will allow you to stop and think about whether or not you want to spend the time going to a particular link.
Building Background Knowledge	If an article refers to something with which you are unfamiliar and you feel the information is important, take the time to ask someone about the topic or do a search to gain additional information.
Synthesizing	As you search, you must synthesize, or put together, the information you are gaining into a coherent whole. Create a system for putting similar information together, such as a graphic organizer or a digital mapping tool.
Generating Questions	Although you will begin with an essential question, this question may change as you gain information. In any case, as researchers, your work will be guided by questions. Start each work session by writing questions that you hope to answer by the end of the period.
Monitoring Comprehension	Although you may perceive online reading to be more engaging than print-based reading, you may still encounter passages, words, or concepts that you don't understand. When this happens, try to decide if the information is valuable. If you think it is, determine how you will comprehend it, such as by rereading, finding another site that contains similar information, or asking your teacher for help.
Determining Importance	The Internet often contains so much information that you may become overwhelmed. One of the reasons that you are working with others is to discuss what is important for your project. You can waste a lot of time chasing "rabbit trails" if you don't ask these questions often: Is this information important for our project? If so, how? If you're not sure, just bookmark the site and come back to it later.

www.snopes.com, a spoof-busting site that can foster lively discussion about the reliability of online information.

Give students a broad topic that has information from several sources, such as Iraq, the Green Party, feminist literature, Albert Einstein, or Hurricane Katrina. Working with a partner, have them critically analyze three different sites on the same topic by using the following criteria:

- What is the source of the site?
- What is the date of the information?
- What do you know about this source?
- How can you find out whether the source is reliable?
    Can the writer be contacted?
    What are the credentials of the person writing the document?
    What is the purpose of the document?
    What words or phrases does the writer use to help you evaluate objectivity?
    Do the links lead you to reputable sites?
- How does one site compare to the others? What criteria did you use to compare sites?
- What is the author's intent in presenting information?

There are many online sites that will help students determine how to evaluate webpages. After they have read several, such as a site from UC Berkeley Library (http://www.lib.berkeley.edu/TeachingLib/Guides/Internet?Evaluate.html) or Cornell University's guidelines (http://www.library.cornell.edu/olinuris/ref/research/webcrit.html), have them create their own set of criteria for evaluating websites. Cornell's site offers a chart of tips on how to interpret accuracy, authority, objectivity, currency, and coverage of web documents. This guide, one students can easily adapt, is simple to read, to the point, and short.

Students can also create a wall chart of reputable and disreputable sites for your content area. Below is a sampling of reputable sites organized by subject area to get them started.

Science

Discovery: http://dsc.discovery.com
Eisenhower National Clearance Center:
    http://www.enc.org:80/

General Chemistry Online:
    http://antoine.frostburg.edu/chem/senese/101/
NatureShift: http://www.natureshift.org/

Math

Eisenhower National Clearinghouse for Mathematics and
    Science Education: http://www.enc.org
Math Forum: http://mathforum.org/
Math Virtual Library:
    http://www.math.fsu.edu/Virtual/index.php

Social Studies

CIA World Factbook:
    http://www.cia.gov/cia/publications/factbook/
Eyewitness History: http://www.eyewitnesstohistory.com/
The History Channel's Historical Speeches:
    http://www.historychannel.com/speeches/
Library of Congress: http://www.loc.gov/
The Smithsonian Homepage: http://www.si.edu/
Sounds of History: http://www.sinbert.com/~history/

English and Language Arts

The Academy of American Poets: http://www.poets.org
Author Studies Homepage:
    http://www2.scholastic.com/teachers/authorsandbooks/
    authorstudies/authorstuidis/jhtml
The Literacy Web: http://www.literacy.unconn.edu
Writer's Web:
    http://writing2.richmond.edu/writing/wweb.html

Primary Sources for Various Subjects

Alta Vista (web, images, video, MP3/audio, news):
    http://www.altavista.com/
FindSounds (sounds, sound effects, and music):
    http://www.findsounds.com
New York Public Library: http://www.nypl.corg/digital/
Our Documents: http://www.ourdocuments.gov/

ONLINE RESEARCH INQUIRY PROJECT

Online research inquiry projects provide meaningful and relevant
opportunities for students to adapt and use critical reading and

thinking skills. Donna Alvermann advocates, "Because many adolescents of the Net Generation will find their own reasons for becoming literate—reasons that go beyond reading to acquire school knowledge or mastery of academic texts—it is important that teachers create sufficient opportunities for students to engage actively in meaningful subject matter projects that both extend and elaborate on the literacy practices they already own and value" (Alvermann, 2001).

Nel Noddings also examined the notion of students actively participating in projects as a way of preparing for our complex society. She lists characteristics such as "willingness to continue learning, an ability to work in teams, patience and skill in problem-solving, intellectual and personal honesty, and a well-developed capacity to think" (Noddings, 2008). Inquiry projects of all types help students develop these important skills in a safe learning lab with a teacher and peers who are available to provide meaningful feedback.

Social interaction or collaboration is equally important for honing reading and computer skills. Those less comfortable with technology learn from others who have more experience, and students' understanding of content is elaborated as they talk about the information they are accessing and make decisions about whether or how it will be used. In fact, in a review of the research on achievement outcomes in improving reading for middle and high school students, the authors concluded that "positive achievement effects were found for instructional-process programs, especially for those involving cooperative learning, and for mixed-methods programs (methods that combine large and small-group instruction with computer activities)" (Slavan, Cheung, Groff, & Lake, 2008). Engaging students in an inquiry project such as the one described below will have long-term benefits for all students.

Getting Started

Make sure students understand the goals of the project before beginning:

- To explore a guiding question in depth through research
- To learn how to use appropriate reading strategies to access information online
- To practice critical reading and thinking

- To refine collaboration and teamwork skills
- To learn how to share information with the class in an engaging and informative manner

This project is an opportunity for students to experience "flow" and become immersed in learning, as described in Chapter 1. As such, students should have as much ownership over the project as possible. Begin the process by having students brainstorm guiding questions related to a broad topic of study, such as tragic heroes in English, skin cancer in science, or a historical event or time period in social studies. You may give students time for reflection by writing or talking in small groups before coming together as a whole class. Then, list on the board every question that students propose, even those that seem far-fetched.

Creating Guiding Questions

Guiding questions reflect a real interest on the part of the student and require advanced thinking skills such as analysis, synthesis, and evaluation. Questions should be open-ended, but may be subject to various perspectives, and the original question will become more refined as students gain knowledge about the topic. The purpose of this project is not to have students find an answer to a question, but to go through a process of analyzing and adapting information in *response* to a question. Following are sample content-area guiding questions.

English Topic: Genres of Literature
- How should graphic novels be used in middle and high school English curriculum?
- What characteristics do Nobel Prize–winning novels share?
- What is poetry?

Social Studies Topic: Industrial Revolution
- In what ways was the Industrial Revolution a turning point for modern society?
- What was the cost of increased productivity on other areas of society, such as child labor or agrarian culture?
- How does the Industrial Revolution compare to the technology revolution?

Science/Geography Topic: Global Warming

- What climate trends over the last century support or discount the theory of global warming?
- How will future global warming affect underdeveloped countries?
- How will the United States' response to global warming change our lifestyle?

After students brainstorm questions, provide them with your edited list of their questions. They should then choose their top three preferences for research. Place students in small groups based on their common choices.

Getting Organized

The first task for each group is to complete a form similar to the one in Figure 7.2 as a way of becoming organized. You should hold a conference with the groups and provide feedback on their plan

FIGURE 7.2. Organization of Online Inquiry Research Project

Group members:

1. What is your guiding question?
2. What will be the focus of your research and reading?

   - What is your purpose?
   - What knowledge are you hoping to gain?
   - Why are you interested in researching this aspect of the topic?

3. How do you intend to begin your online research? List key words, sites, or online communication tools you think will be helpful.
4. How will the work be divided among group members?
5. How will you synthesize the information that you collect?
6. How will you know your sources are reliable and accurate?
7. How do you plan to report your new learning to the class? (Examples: visual presentation, PowerPoint, digital video composition, oral report, booklet for class library.) As you research, you may decide that one type of presentation lends itself better to your topic than what you had originally planned.
8. How will you monitor your progress?
9. When will you meet with your teacher to gain feedback?

FIGURE 7.3. Online Research Inquiry Project

Website Form

URL or online communication:

Source and author:

- Provide a summary of the most important points from this site.
- Write quotes you will use from this site. Include the names and credentials of the sources.
- What new vocabulary did you learn from this site?
- Evaluate the site: How do you know the information is accurate and reliable? Be specific.
- Rate the usefulness of the site: 1 being the worst, 10 being the best. Write a brief explanation of your rating.

prior to their logging on, as well as at designated times throughout the process. Set a timeframe for completion, but tell students that they are responsible for pacing their progress, making decisions about the sources they use, setting tasks for group members, and deciding how how they will present their findings to the class.

Evaluating Websites

For every website or online communication that students use, they should fill out a form similar to Figure 7.3 to be turned in with their presentation. The group may choose one student as a recorder, but every member will contribute to and be responsible for completing the form.

Self-Assessment

Students should complete a self-assessment similar to Figure 7.4 to help them assume responsibility for their part of the work and guide them in reflecting on their own learning.

FIGURE 7.4. Self-Assessment of Online Inquiry Research Project

Guiding Question:

Name:

Group Members:

1. How would you answer the above question?
2. Describe the process that your group engaged in during your work sessions.
3. Describe *specifically* how you contributed to the group's work.
4. What did you learn from this project in the following areas? Give examples to support your statements.
    *   Working with classmates
    *   Using features of the computer
    *   Accessing information on the Internet
    *   Participating in online communication
    *   Determining which information is most important
    *   Evaluating online sources for accuracy and reliability
    *   Synthesizing information into a report
    *   Presenting information to the class
5. In what ways are reading print and reading online alike? Different?
6. What did you learn that will be most helpful to you in the future?

INTEGRATING CONCEPTS

Online research inquiry projects give students the opportunity to use skills that foster independence while gaining important content-area knowledge. The more students use the Internet to gain or confirm information with the support and feedback of a teacher and peers, the more proficient they will become at reading all texts—visual, print-based, and online.

Principles for Online Reading

- Show students how online reading and print-based reading are alike and different.
- Allow students opportunities to navigate networks to locate and synthesize relevant information.
- Teach students how to critically evaluate the usefulness and reliability of online information.
- Provide students with tasks that require their use of online communication tools.
- Engage students in online inquiry research projects to practice and sharpen collaborative online reading skills.

Quote for Reflection

"I think it's fair to say that personal computers have become the most empowering tool we've ever created. They're tools of communication, they're tools of creativity, and they can be shaped by their user."

—Bill Gates

Study Group Resources

Alvermann, D. (Ed.). (2004). *Adolescents and literacies in a digital world*. New York: Peter Lang.

Leu, D. J., Leu, D. D., & Coiro, J. (2004). *Teaching with the internet K–12: New literacies for new times* (4th ed.). Norwood, MA: Christopher-Gordon.

Warlick, D. (2004). *Re-defining literacy for the 21st Century*. Worthington, OH: Linworth.

CHAPTER 8

Expanding Reading Across Content Areas

F OR MANY YEARS AS BOTH A middle and high school teacher, I began the school year trying to pull together as many resources as possible related to the topics I was to teach. I can remember digging through the book room looking for books that had been discarded or spare copies of textbooks that hadn't been "adopted" so I could use selections from them to supplement the official text I had been given. Like a greedy miser, I stockpiled these resources the way others might hoard dry-erase markers. The most valuable part of my stash was an extensive classroom library of fiction, nonfiction, poetry, magazines, books on tape, and files of online articles.

Diverse texts continue to be central to my literacy work with teachers and students because I know that we don't just write, we write *something*; we don't just read, we read *something*; and we don't just teach, we teach *something*. That something is represented by words and images interwoven through the content-area subjects in all sorts of texts. I also know that my chances of getting kids turned on to reading are far more likely when engaging, suitable, relevant texts are available.

I will always remember a 10th-grade student in my reading class who told me he had never read a book in his life. He was, therefore, not enthusiastic about my independent reading program: 15 minutes of silent reading each day. Finally, he chose James Dickey's *Deliverance* from my well-stocked classroom library. Although the novel was probably not right for most of my students, this particular young man couldn't put it down. When he finished it, he asked to go to the library to check out something else by "that great author." Unfortunately, he returned appalled; the only other books he found by Dickey were volumes of poetry.

This student had been exposed to reading strategies, test prep worksheets, vocabulary exercises, and packaged programs for many years. Not surprisingly, it was a *text* that engaged him to such a degree that he became independent in his use of strategies and skills. In addition, he discovered that reading is more than an eye-movement exercise that will guarantee a diploma.

This final chapter, then, will emphasize how texts nurture engagement, vocabulary, and deep, critical reading.

DIVERSE TEXTS

The *Reading Next Report* affirms this book's philosophy with one of 15 key elements of effective adolescent literacy programs titled simply "diverse texts." The report defines such texts as materials that represent a wide range of topics at a variety of reading levels. The report advises, "In addition to using appropriate grade-level textbooks that may already be available in the classroom, it is crucial to have a range of texts in the classroom that link to multiple ability levels and connect to students' background experiences" (Biancarosa & Snow, 2004, p. 18). This echoes the position statement from the International Reading Association's Commission on Adolescent

Literacy: "Adolescents deserve access to a wide variety of reading material that they can and want to read" (Moore, Bean, Birdyshaw, & Rycik, 1999, p. 4).

The National Council of Teachers of English (2004) offers a similar "Call to Action." It contends that adolescents need "sustained experiences with diverse texts in a variety of genres" and "multiple perspectives on real-life experiences" (p. 3). The document provides a rationale in addition to a directive: "Although many of these texts will be required by the curriculum, others should be self-selected and of high interest to the reader. Wide, independent reading develops fluency, builds vocabulary and knowledge of text structures, and offers readers the experiences they need to read and construct meaning with more challenging texts. Text should be broadly viewed to include print, electronic, and visual media" (p. 4).

It is also important that students read multiple texts to develop a critical perspective—a "social, cultural, and ecological understanding" that is often missing in sanitized textbooks (Behrman, 2006, p. 492).

As we build a framework for critical, strategic reading with the important components of engagement, vocabulary, and effective instructional practices, the role of supplemental texts cannot be overstated. Perhaps Ivey and Fisher said it best in their book *Creating Literacy-Rich Schools for Adolescents* (2006): "All the strategy instruction in the world will not help build the skill and motivation to read when students do not have access to an abundance of interesting, manageable texts" (p. 92).

SUSTAINED SILENT READING (SSR)

The implication for Sustained Silent Reading (SSR) or independent reading in content areas is significant, especially considering the importance that background knowledge and vocabulary play in comprehension of academic texts. If you doubt the effectiveness of the practice, consider Hoover High School in San Diego, California. Douglas Fisher, Nancy Frey, and principal Douglas Williams describe impressive results in student achievement when the staff instituted SSR as one of the components in its plan for improvement. The school was the lowest-performing school in the city of San Diego and among the lowest-performing high schools in the state of California. In 5 years, students increased their reading achievement by an average of 2.4 years, and Hoover had the highest gain in the city on the state accountability test (Fisher, Frey, & Williams, 2004, p. 159). It follows that when students' reading skills increase, they are better able to comprehend content-area texts. Nancie Atwell reported, "The major predictor of academic success is the amount of time students spend reading. In fact, the top 5% of U.S. students read up to 144 more books than the kids in the bottom 5%" (Atwell, 2007, p. 107).

School-Wide and Content-Area SSR

There are two types of sustained silent reading. One initiative includes school-wide reading at a designated time that includes all students and often staff, the approach that Hoover High implemented. The other type of SSR occurs in classrooms, where teachers provide time for students to participate in independent, self-selected reading. Steve Gardiner, author of *Building Student Literacy Through Sustained Silent Reading* (2005), reports that dozens of studies show that SSR can improve students' vocabulary, comprehension, and engagement. Gardiner's own research found that students who engaged in SSR earned higher grades. In another study of high school students participating in SSR in English classes, researchers found that students gained an average of 1.9 grade levels in reading growth while those who did not participate gained an average of 0.5 grade level (Kornelly & Smith, 1993).

Consider conducting your own action research project, perhaps with a colleague, to determine the effect of SSR on your students' achievement. Teach two classes of comparable students the same unit—for example, the Westward Expansion in American history or literature of the American West in English. In one class, teach the content as you traditionally do. In the other class, provide students with a variety of texts related to the topic, such as texts about the California Gold Rush, the Lewis and Clark expedition, or the displacement of the American Indians. Give students a designated time to read several times a week. Assess students at the end of the unit to determine the effect that SSR had on content-area knowledge. Keep in mind that research indicates greater results when the practice is sustained over 1 year (Gardiner, 2005).

Implementing Content-Area SSR

The procedure for creating a Sustained Silent Reading program is simple.

1. Students will choose materials from your class library (or bring texts from home) that are related to the unit of study. They should be allowed 15 to 20 minutes two or three times a week for silent reading.
2. The room should be quiet during SSR.
3. The teacher will move around the room and talk quietly with students about what they are reading or provide suggestions for future reading. This is an ideal time to get to know students or build background knowledge.
4. At the end of the reading time, you may opt to have students do nothing more than put their books away and prepare for class, discuss what they have read with a partner, or ask students to respond briefly to what they have read. A log such as the one in Figure 8.1 may be used for this purpose.

CLASSROOM LIBRARIES

The most effective way to provide students with a wide variety of accessible texts is to create a classroom library. Although money is certainly an issue in these days of budget cuts, there are ways of building a strong classroom library without turning over your salary for books.

FIGURE 8.1. Sustained Silent Reading Log

Name _____

Date	Title of Book or Article	Pages Read	Response

Finding Money

- Administrators will often find money for classroom libraries if they are convinced of their importance. In many schools, for example, Title I money, school improvement funds, or "rainy day" savings are available to purchase books.
- Ask if textbook funds can be used to buy books for classroom libraries. Show the district curriculum director research regarding increased reading comprehension through "diverse texts" cited throughout this book and request seed money to begin your classroom library.
- Grants are great ways to create classroom libraries. The criteria for almost any academic grant include reading, so begin at the school level, perhaps with Parent-Teacher Advisory grants, and go from there. Giant corporations such as Wal-Mart as well as local business or associations, such as the local bar association, will often provide money for books as a part of their community goodwill effort. Bookstores such as Barnes & Noble may also sponsor events such as school-based or in-store book fairs, with the school receiving a percentage of sales.
- Initiate a school-wide book drive, with students as organizers. Take the books that are not appropriate to a used bookstore in exchange for others that are more desirable.
- If all else fails, ask your media specialist to create a cart of books for your subject area as a temporary classroom library.

Finding Time

Teachers often mistakenly believe that maintaining a classroom library will take up time that is needed for planning lessons, grading papers, or conferencing with students. A well-organized classroom library practically runs itself. In every class, assign a student to be in charge of the classroom library, recording checkouts and returns, and staying on top of "overdues." Likewise, as you or students find magazine, newspaper, or online articles related to your subject area, give them to the "media" student to place in a file drawer for check-out. Once your classroom library begins to take shape, you will find that it almost magically comes alive with all sorts of texts.

Finding Texts

One of my favorite ways to find content-area, supplemental texts is to browse the "bargain" section of large bookstores to note the reading level, nonprint features, and overall appeal of a book. Cyberbrowsing is also an option. I have found award-winning young adult books for as little as a dollar and nonfiction books rich with compelling primary documents in bargain sections for adults. Most bookstores will also offer teachers a nice discount for books to be used in the classroom. Before heading out to scan acres of books, however, you might want to review resources such as the following to help you make wise choices.

- The Journal of the Assembly on Literature for Adolescents, in conjunction with the National Council of Teachers of English, publishes a journal devoted to young adult (YA) literature, the *ALAN Review.* You can also access their website at www.alan-ya.org/.
- The International Reading Association offers book lists in many categories at www.ira.org. They also sponsor Choice Awards for Young Adults, where 30 books are selected each year by teams of teenage reviewers. The books chosen for this award for the last several years can be accessed at http://www.ira.org/resources/tools/choices_young_adults.html.
- The National Council for Social Studies booklist is available at www.socialstudies.org/resources/notable/. These books are written primarily for children in grades K–8.
- The National Science Teachers Association offers a list of outstanding science trade books for children at http://www.nsta.org/publications/ostb/.
- Great Books for Children and Young Adults can be accessed at www.richiespicks.com/. You (or your students) can sign up for Richie Partington's online newsletters in which he provides excellent reviews of new books.
- Voice of Youth Advocates (VOYA) offers extensive reviews of young adult materials at www.voya.com/.
- The Children's Book Committee of Bank Street College provides a list of teen books for mature readers at http://www.bnkst.edu/bookcom/teen.html.

- The American Library Association offers extensive current booklists and book awards in categories ranging from graphic novels to outstanding books for college-bound students at http://www.ala.org/ala/yalsa/booklistsawards/booklistsbook.cfm.
- www.teenreads.com offers author talks, reviews, book clubs, podcasts, and an e-newsletter about "cool and new" books.

CURRENT EVENTS PERIODICALS

Current events magazines are valuable ways to build students' background knowledge, reinforce reading and writing skills, and give students a different perspective on a variety of topics. I strongly suggest that the school purchase a class set of current events periodicals, such as *Time* or *Newsweek*, at the reduced student subscription rate offered by publishers for school use. As with books in series, students become familiar with certain aspects of the magazines and anticipate favorite features, such as letters to the editor, music/movie reviews, and even a "numbers" column in *Time*. Students also discuss articles with parents, teachers, and peers as they come to understand the intricacies of events that are a part of their larger world. With such periodicals, students may become *enthusiastic*, critical readers of nonfiction. When Dale Earnhardt, the popular race car driver, was pictured on the cover of *Time* after he was killed in a crash, many of my students, particularly males who "hated reading," devoured every word of the long article and asked to take the magazine home.

The value of such periodicals is that teachers often don't know which piece will be the one that captivates students. Such periodicals are also the ultimate differentiated teaching tool, even for middle school students, and the variety of visual features such as charts, graphs, political cartoons, and photographs is timelier than those found in textbooks. In addition, magazines now supplement many articles with online features and blogs.

Consider having the school's class set of magazines delivered to the media specialist or reading coach, who can copy the table of contents and place it in teachers' boxes. Teachers may then request the class set if they find articles that are pertinent to units of study.

TEXT SETS

Text sets are collections of texts of various genres that are related to a common theme. The type of texts included in a text set depends upon the topic and purpose of study, but anything is fair game as long as students are reading and exploring, often in small groups. The mixture of independent reading and collaboration also allows students to practice many of the reading skills described in earlier chapters, such as generating questions, recognizing text structure, determining importance, and conceptualizing vocabulary.

How to Use Text Sets

Think about topics you currently teach that have multiple components or those that could be expanded. Examples include the following:

- Themes in English, such as love or greed
- Time periods or events in social studies, such as the Depression or the Cuban Missile Crisis
- Topics in science, such as brain research or bacteria
- Units in math, such as measurement or ratio
- Biographies in any subject, such as famous artists, writers, politicians, or scientists
- Current topics related to your subject area, such as local recycling projects in a community service class, nutrition in health class, or school shootings in current events classes
- Topics for special events such as for science, social studies, or math fairs, as well as for Black History or National Poetry Month

Text sets can be used to increase background knowledge, extend learning on a topic, or interest students in independent reading. They may also serve as resources for exploring essential questions, developing oral presentations, or prompting collaborative study. A sample lesson for middle school students on how to use text sets can be found at Read-Write Think (http://www.readwritethink.org/lessons/lesson_view.asp?id=305).

Sample Text Set on "Epidemics"

Figure 8.2 provides a list of texts that could be included in a text set for the study of epidemics in a science, English, or sociology class. Notice that the texts span reading levels, genres, and sources, including online and visual resources. Think of a unit in your curriculum that would lend itself to independent and small-group study through text sets, and work with colleagues within your department or across the curriculum to design sets for content topics. Text sets may begin small but often grow into wonderfully diverse sources of information. Students, too, enjoy adding to the text sets once they become "experts" on the topic.

INTEGRATING CONCEPTS

Educators are fond of saying that there is no silver bullet for creating proficient readers, and this is evident when you walk through the exhibit halls of national conferences. Expensive programs and texts that guarantee "reading achievement" abound in every conceivable color and shape with impressive extras. Perhaps the closest we can come to that elusive bullet is simply to offer students an abundance of text—print, visual, and electronic —on a variety of topics and allow the magic of reading to work its spell.

Principles for Expanding Reading Across Content Areas

- Provide students with diverse texts, including print, electronic, and visual media, those that represent a wide range of topics at a variety of reading levels.
- Incorporate sustained silent reading to increase content knowledge and build independent reading skills.
- Make texts accessible by creating classroom libraries.
- Provide current events periodicals to help students make connections, build background knowledge, and reinforce reading and vocabulary skills.
- Use text sets to extend knowledge in content areas and provide information in a variety of formats.

FIGURE 8.2. Text Set for the Study of Epidemics

Code Orange by Caroline Cooney
- Easy-to-read young adult novel about a teen assigned to do a report on smallpox who comes to believe he has contracted the virus

An American Plague: The True and Terrifying Story of the Yellow Fever Epidemic of 1793 by Jim Murphy
- Nonfiction account of the spread of the yellow fever through Philadelphia, complete with primary documents and medical details

EyeWitnesstoHistory.com
http://www.eyewitnesstohistory.com/pfyellowfever.htm
- Website containing true accounts written by people who survived the yellow fever attacks in Philadelphia

Year of Wonders: A Novel of the Plague by Geraldine Brooks
- Novel for proficient readers about the 1666 plague in England told from the point of view of a housemaid

Time Magazine: February 23, 1998—"The Flu Hunters"
http://www.time.com/time/magazine/article/0,9171,987857,00.html
- The cover story of this issue is on the flu virus

The Last Town on Earth: A Novel by Thomas Mullen
(Also available for Amazon Kindle, Amazon's wireless reading device)
- A fast-paced, best-selling novel with a young male protagonist who tells the story of a small town that quarantined itself against the flu epidemic of 1918

Demon in the Freezer by Richard Preston
- Nonfiction account of the history of smallpox as well as an analysis of its potential as a biological weapon

Library of Congress—American Memory:
http://memory.loc.gov/cgi-bin/query
- Early motion picture showing San Francisco's Chinatown in 1900 when cases of bubonic plague were found due to overcrowding

Fever 1793 by Laurie Halse Anderson
- Easy-to-read young adult novel with a female protagonist who survives the 1793 plague

Harper's Magazine, "We Are Not Immune: Influenza, SARS, and the collapse of public health" by Ronald J. Glasser, M.D. July, 2004
- Comprehensive essay about the U.S. Public Health Department's ability to deal with epidemics

New York Times Deadly Invaders: Virus Outbreaks Around the World, From Marburg Fever to Avian Flu by Denise Grady
- Young adult nonfiction written by a *New York Times* reporter who researches viral epidemics

Quote for Reflection

"It is like the rubbing of two sticks together to make a fire, the act of reading, an improbably pedestrian task that leads to heat and light."

—Anna Quindlen

Resources for Study Groups

Atwell, N. (2007). *The reading zone: How to help kids become skilled, passionate, habitual, critical readers*. New York: Scholastic.

Lesesne, T. (2003). *Making the match: The right book for the right reader at the right time, grades 4–12*. Portland, ME: Stenhouse.

Richison, J., Hernandez, A., & Carter, M. (2006). *Theme-sets for secondary students: How to scaffold core literature*. Portland, NH: Heinemann.

Zarnowski, M. (2006). *Making sense of history: Using high-quality literature and hands-on experiences to build content knowledge*. New York: Scholastic.

Margaret Meek said, "What is it to be literate? We were always in dialogue with others—those who taught us to read, those for whom we wrote, who lent us books, shaped our preferences, encouraged us, forbade us even. They were dead poets, living authors, cynical critics." I would add "teachers" to Meek's list. As teachers, we have the opportunity and obligation to change the world for our students through texts that are infinite in their power and promise. But it's not just the abundance and variety of texts that make us fortunate to be teaching and learning in the 21st century. There is an unprecedented national focus on content-area literacy, along with reliable research to guide our instructional practices. Our roles as teachers have changed over the last few decades from lecturers to coaches and from providing information to facilitating the acquisition of knowledge. Our students have changed as well, from print-centric readers to multi-faceted users of digital literacy. Nevertheless, we are all on this journey together. It is a beautiful partnership in secondary schools—teachers and students *using* literacy as a means of exploring the incredible amount of information at our fingertips, our common experiences in a rapidly evolving society, and the diverse ways that we can now read.

Resources

Fiction

Brooks, G. (2002). *Year of wonders: A novel of the plague.* New York: Penguin.
Brown, D. (2006). *The Da Vinci code.* Port Moody, BC: Anchor.
Dickey, J. (1994). *Deliverance.* New York: Delta.
Frazier, C. (2006). *Cold Mountain.* New York: Atlantic Monthly Press.
Frank, A. (1993). *Anne Frank: The diary of a young girl.* New York: Bantam.
Homer. (2006). *The odyssey.* New York: Penguin Classics.
Miller, A. (1996). *The crucible.* New York: Penguin.
Mullen, T. (2008). *The last town on earth: A novel.* New York: Random House.
Philbrick, N. (2007). *Mayflower: A story of courage, community and war.* New York: Penguin.
Orwell, G. (2004). *Animal farm.* New York: Signet Classics.
Steinbeck, J. (2002). *Of mice and men.* New York: Penguin.
Wiesel, E. (2006). *Night.* New York: Hill and Wang.

Films

Burns, K. (Director), & Burns, K. & Burnes, R. (Producers). (1990). *The Civil War: A Film by Ken Burns.* USA: Public Broadcasting System.
Grazer, B. (Producer), & Howard, R. (Director). (2001). *A Beautiful Mind.* USA: Universal Pictures.
Kates, N., & Singer, B. (Producers & Directors). (2003). *Brother Outsider: The Life of Bayard Rustin.*
McDonald, K. (Producer & Director). (2006). *The Last King of Scotland.* UK: DNA Films.
Nelson, S. (Producer & Director). (2003). *American Experience: The Murder of Emmett Till.* USA: WGBH Educational Foundation.
Penn, S. (Producer & Director). (2007). *Into the Wild.* USA: Paramount.
Peterson, W. (Producer & Director). (2004). *Troy.* USA: Warner Brothers Pictures.
Spielberg, S. (Producer & Director). (1996). *Survivors of the Holocaust.* USA: Turner Home Entertainment.

Graphic Novels

Lemelman, M. (2007). *Mendel's daughter: A memoir.* New York: Free Press.
Spiegelman, A. (1986). *The complete Maus: A survivor's tale.* New York: Pantheon Books.

Nonfiction

Armstrong, J. (2005). *Photo by Brady: A picture of the Civil War.* New York: Antheneum Books for Young Readers.

Grady, D. (2006). *New York Times deadly invaders: Virus outbreaks around the world, from Marburg fever to avian flu.* Boston: Kingfisher.

Graham, R. L., & Gill, D. T. (1991). *Dove.* New York: Harper Paperbacks.

Hari, D. (2008). *The translator: A tribesman's memoir of Darfur.* New York: Random House.

Mankoff, R., & Buckley, C. (2000). *New Yorker's book of political cartoons.* Princeton, NJ: Bloomberg Press.

Moore, E. (2004). *Hey, kidz! buy this book: A radical primer on corporate and governmental propaganda and artistic activism for short people.* New York: Soft Skull Press.

Murphy, J. (2003). *An American plague: The true and terrifying story of the yellow fever epidemic of 1793.* New York: Clarion Books.

Preston, R. (2003). *Demon in the freezer.* New York: Fawcett.

Surowiecki, J. (2005). *The wisdom of crowds.* New York: Random House.

Till-Mobley, M., & Benson, C. (2004). *Death of innocence: The story of the hate crime that changed America.* New York: One World.

Verhoeven, R., Van der Rol, R., Quindlen, A., & Langham, T. (1995). *Anne Frank: Beyond the diary: A photographic remembrance.* New York: Puffin.

Wisenthal, S. (1998). *The sunflower: On the possibilities and limits of forgiveness.* New York: Schocken.

Picture Books for Older Readers

Alverez, J. (2000). *The secret footprints.* New York: Knopf.

Borden, L. (2004). *Sea clocks: The story of longitude.* New York: Margaret K. McElderry Books.

Bunting, E. (1999). *Smoky night.* Orlando, FL: Voyager Books.

Deedy, C. A. (2007). *Martina, the beautiful cochroach: A Cuban folktale.* Atlanta: Peachtree.

Deedy, C. A. (2000). *The yellow star of Denmark.* Atlanta: Peachtree.

Myers, W. D. (2003). *Malcolm X: A fire burning brightly.* New York: Amistad.

Myers, W. D. (2002). *Patrol: An American solider in Vietnam.* New York: HarperCollins Children's Books.

Nikola-Lisa, W. (2006). *How we are smart.* New York: Lee and Low Books.

Nivola, C. (2008). *Planting the trees of Kenya: The story of Wangari Maathai.* New York: Frances Foster Books.

Popov, N. (1995). *Why?* New York: North-South Books.

Rubin, S. (2000). *Fireflies in the dark: The story of Friedl Dicker-Brandeis and the children of Terezin.* New York: Holiday House.

Smith, C. R. (2007). *Twelve rounds to glory: The story of Muhammad Ali.* Cambridge, MA: Candlewick.

Tompert, A. (2003). *Joan of Arc: Heroine of France.* Honesdale, PA: Boyds Mills Press.

Young Adult Literature

Anderson, L. H. (2002). *Fever, 1793.* New York: Aladdin Paperbacks.

Anderson, M. T. (2006). *The astonishing life of Octavian Nothing, traitor to the nation, Vol. 1: The pox party.* Cambridge, MA: Candlewick.

Bloor, E. (2008). *London calling.* New York: Knopf Books for Young Readers.

Boyne, J. (2006). *The boy in the striped pajamas.* Oxford: David Fickling Books.

Cooney, C. (2007). *Code orange.* New York: Laurel Leaf.

Donnelly, J. (2004). *A northern light.* Boston: Harcourt Paperbacks.

Fogelin, A. (2002). *Crossing Jordan.* Atlanta: Peachtree, Jr.

Haddon, M. (2004). *The curious incident of the dog in the night-time.* New York: Vintage.

Hobbs, W. (2007). *Crossing the wire.* New York: Harper Trophy.

Klass, D. (2002). *You don't know me.* New York: HarperCollins.

Lowry, L. (1990). *Number the stars.* New York: Yearling.

McCormick, P. (2008). *Sold.* New York: Hyperion.

Mickaelsen, B. (2004). *Tree girl, a novel.* New York: Harper Tempest.

Myers, S. (2006). *Twilight.* New York: Little Brown and Company.

Myers, W. D. (1988). *Fallen angels.* New York: Scholastic.

Parks, L. S. (2004). *When my name was Keoko.* New York: Clarion.

Rees, C. (2002). *Witch child.* Cambridge, MA: Candlewick.

Riordan, R. (2006). *The lightning thief (Percy Jackson and the Olympians, Book 1).* New York: Miramax.

Westerfeld, S. (2005). *Uglies.* New York: Scholastic Trade.

Websites

The Academy of American Poets: http://www.poets.org

Alta Vista (web, images, video, MP3/audio, news): http://www.altavista.com/)

American Library Association: www.ala.org

Author Studies Homepage: http://www2.scholastic.com/teachers/authorsandbooks/authorstudies/authorstuidis/jhtml

Choices Book List—Young Adults' Choices: www.ira.org/resources/tools/choices_young_adults.html

CIA World Factbook: http://www.cia.gov/cia/publications/factbook/

Comic Book Projects: www.comicbookproject.org

Cornell University's Guidelines: http://www.library.cornell.edu/olinuris/ref/research/webcrit.html

Discovery: http://dsc.discovery.com

Eisenhower National Clearinghouse for Mathematics and Science Education: http://www.enc.org

Eyewitness to History: http://www.eyewitnesstohistory.com/

Findsounds: http://www.findsounds.com

General Chemistry Online: http://antoine.frostburg.edu/chem/senese/101/

Graphic Organizers: www.graphicorganizers.com

The History Channel's Historical Speeches:
    http://www.historychannel.com/speeches
Howard Gardner: www.howardgardner.com
International Reading Association: www.ira.org
The Journal of the Assembly on Literature for Adolescents:
    www.alan-ya.org/
Library of Congress: http://www.loc.gov/
Library of Congress, American Memory: http://memory.loc.gov/
The Literacy Web: http://www.literacy.unconn.edu
Literature Circles: www.literatuecircles.com
Math Forum: http://mathforum.org/
Math Virtual Library: http://www.math.fsu.edu/Virtual/index.php
NASA: www.nasa.gov/
The National Council for Social Studies booklist:
    www.socialstudies.org/resources/notable/
National Issues Forum: www.nifi.org
National Paideia Center: www.paideia.org
National Public Radio, The Math Guy:
    http://www.stanford.edu/~kdevlin/MathGuy.html
The National Science Teachers Association science trade books:
    http://www.nsta.org/publications/ostb/
NatureShift: http://www.natureshift.org/
New York Public Library: http://www.nypl.corg/digital/
Oakland Museum of California, photographs by Dorothea Lange:
    http://www.oac.cdlib.org/
Our Documents: http://www.ourdocuments.gov
Phil Bradley's website (fake or spoof websites):
    http://www.philb.com/fakesites.htm
Political Cartoons: www.politicalcartoons.com
Read-Write-Think: www.readwritethink.org
Read-Write-Think Lesson on Textsets:
    http://www.readwritethink.org/lessons/lesson_view.asp?id=305
Read-Write-Think Lesson on Propaganda Techniques:
    http://www.readwritethink.org/lessons/lesson_view.asp?id=405
Richie's Picks: www.richiespicks.com/
The Smithsonian Homepage: http://www.si.edu/
Snopes (a spoof-busting site): www.snopes.com
Sounds of History: http://www.sinbert.com/~history/
UC Berkeley Library Guide:
    http://www.lib.berkeley.edu/TeachingLib/Guides/
    Internet?Evaluate.html
United States Holocaust Memorial Museum: www.ushmm.org
Voice of Youth Advocates (VOYA): www.voya.com/
Writer's Web: http://writing2.richmond.edu/writing/wweb.html

References

Alliance for Excellent Education. (2007). *High school teaching for the twenty-first century: Preparing students for college.* Washington, DC: Author.

Alvermann, D. E. (1986). *Graphic organizers: Cuing devices for comprehending and remembering main ideas.* In J. F. Bauman (Ed.), *Teaching main idea comprehension* (pp. 210–226). Newark, DE: International Reading Association.

Alvermann, D. E. (2001). *Effective literacy instruction for adolescents* [Executive summary and paper commissioned by the National Reading Conference]. Chicago, IL: National Reading Conference.

Alvermann, D. E. (2003). *Seeing themselves as capable and engaged readers: Adolescents and remediated instruction.* Naperville, IL: Learning Point Associates.

Alvermann, D. E., & Moore, D. W. (1991). *Secondary school reading.* In R. Barr, M. L. Kamil, P. B. Mosenthal, & P. D. Pearson (Eds.), *Handbook of reading research* (Vol. 2, pp. 951–983). New York: Longmann.

Amrein, A. L., & Berliner, D. C. (2002). *High-stakes testing, uncertainty, and student learning.* Retrieved July 23, 2008, from http://epaa.asu.edu/epaa/v10n18/

Anderson, R. C., & Pearson, P. D. (1984). *A schematheoretic view of basic processes in reading.* In P. D. Pearson (Ed.), *Handbook of reading research* (Vol. 1, pp. 255–317). New York: Longman.

Atwell, N. (2007). *The reading zone: How to help kids become skilled, passionate, habitual, critical readers.* New York: Scholastic.

Baca, J. S. (1990). *"Immigrants in our own land" and selected early poems.* New York: New Directions.

Beck, I. L., & McKeown, M. G. (2006). *Improving comprehension with questioning the author: A fresh and expanded view of a powerful approach.* New York: Scholastic.

Beck, I. L., McKeown, M. G., & Kucan, L. (2002). *Bringing words to life: Robust vocabulary instruction.* New York: Guilford.

Behrman, E. H. (2006). Teaching about language, power, and text: A review of classroom practices that support critical literacy. *Journal of Adolescent & Adult Literacy, 49,* 490–498.

Biancarosa, G., & Snow, C. E. (2004). *Reading next—A vision for action and research in middle and high school literacy: A report from Carnegie Corporation of New York.* Washington, DC: Alliance for Excellent Education.

Billmeyer, R., & Barton, M. L. (2002). *Teaching reading in the content areas: If not me, then who?* (2nd ed.). Aurora, CO: Mid-Continent Research for Education and Learning.

Branan, N. (2008). She never forgets a face. *Scientific American Mind, 19*(3), 7.

Cambourne, B. (1995). Toward an educationally relevant theory of literacy learning: Twenty years of inquiry. *The Reading Teacher, 49,* 182–190.

Cambourne, B. (2008, February 4–7). 20 years of educational research and what has been learned. Available at http://www.rcowen.com/TLNSolutionsBCambourne1.htm

Carr, K., Buchannan, D., Wentz, J., Weiss, M., & Brant, K. (2001). Not just for the primary grades: A bibliography of picture books for secondary content teachers. *Journal of Adolescent and Adult Literacy, 45*(2), 146–153.

Carter, B. (2007). *Building literacy connections with graphic novels: Page by page, panel by panel.* Urbana, IL: National Council of Teachers of English.

Clay, M. (2002). *An observation survey of early literacy achievement.* Portsmouth, NH: Heinemann.

Coiro, J. (2003). Reading comprehension on the internet. *Reading Online.* Retrieved May 14, 2008, from www.readingonline.org/electronic/elec_index.asp?HREF=/electronic/rt/2-03_Column

Coiro, J. (2005). Making sense of online text. *Educational Leadership, 63*(2), 30–35.

Copeland, M. (2005). *Socratic circles: Fostering critical and creative thinking in middle and high school.* Portland, ME: Stenhouse.

Costa, A. (2008). The thought-filled curriculum. *Educational Leadership, 65*(5), 20–24.

Costa, A. L., & Kallick, B. (2000). *Habits of mind: A developmental series.* Alexandria, VA: Association for Supervision and Curriculum Development.

Darling-Hammond, L. (2008, March). Teacher development and how it impacts school redesign. Speech presented at the conference of the National Urban Alliance, Albany.

Darling-Hammond, L., & Bransford, J. (Eds.). (2005). *Preparing teachers for a changing world: What teachers should learn and be able to do.* San Francisco: Jossey-Bass.

Dozier, C., Johnston, P., & Rogers, R. (2006). *Critical literacy/critical teaching.* New York: Teachers College Press.

Fisher, D., Frey, N., & Williams, D. (2004). Five years later: The outcomes of a schoolwide approach to increasing achievement in an urban high school. In D. Strickland & D. Alvermann (Eds.), *Building the literacy achievement gap, grades 4–12* (pp. 147–163). New York: Teachers College Press.

Gardiner, S. (2005). *Building student literacy through sustained silent reading.* Alexandria, VA: Association for Supervision and Curriculum Development.

Gardner, H. (1991). *The unschooled mind: How children think & how schools should teach.* New York: Basic Books.

Gardner, H. (2003, April). Multiple intelligences after twenty years. Paper presented at the annual meeting of the American Educational Research Association, Chicago.

Gardner, H., & Hatch, T. (1989). Multiple intelligences go to school: Educational implications of the theory of multiple intelligences. *Educational Researcher, 18*(8), 4–9.

Glasser, R. (2004, July). We are not immune: Influenza, SARS, and the collapse of public health. *Harper's Magazine,* pp. 35–42.

Greenleaf, C., Brown, W., & Litman, C. (2004). Apprenticing urban youth to science literacy. In D. Strickland & D. Alvermann (Eds.), *Building the literacy achievement gap, grades 4–12* (pp. 200–226). New York: Teachers College Press.

Grossman, L. (2008, April 24). Stephanie Meyer: A new J. K. Rowling. *Time.* Retrieved May 18, 2008, from http://www.time.com/time/magazine/article/0,9171,1734838,00.html

Guthrie, J. T. (2001). Contexts for engagement and motivation in reading. *Reading Online, 4*(8). Retrieved May 19, 2008, from http://www.readingonline.org/articles/art_index.asp?HREF=/articles/handbook/guthrie/index.html

Guthrie, J. T., & Anderson, E. (1999). Engagement in reading: Processes of motivated, strategic, knowledgeable, social readers. In J. T. Guthrie & D. E. Alvermann (Eds.), *Engaged reading: Processes, practices, and policy pmplications* (pp. 17–45). New York: Teachers College Press.

Guthrie, J. T., & Wigfield, A. (2000). Engagement and motivation in reading. In M. L. Kamil, P. B. Mosenthal, P. D. Pearson, & R. Barr (Eds.), *Handbook of reading research* (Vol. 3, pp. 403–422). Mahwah, NJ: Erlbaum.

Heimlich, J. E., & Pittelman, S. D. (1986). *Semantic mapping: Classroom applications.* Newark, DE: International Reading Association.

Heller, R., & Greenleaf, C. (2007). *Literacy instruction in the content areas: Getting to the core of middle and high school improvement.* Washington, DC: Alliance for Excellent Education.

Herber, H. L. (1978). *Teaching reading in the content areas.* Englewood Cliffs, NJ: Prentice Hall.

International Reading Association. (2001). *Integrating literacy and technology in the curriculum: A position statement of the International Reading Association.* Newark, DE: Author.

Irvin, J. L., Buehl, D. R., & Klemp, R. M. (2003). *Reading and the high school student: Strategies to enhance literacy.* Boston: Allyn and Bacon.

Ivey, G., & Fisher, D. (2006). *Creating literacy-rich schools for adolescents.* Alexandria, VA: Association for Supervision and Curriculum Development.

Johnson, D. D., & Pearson, P. D. (1984). *Teaching reading vocabulary* (2nd ed.). New York: Holt, Rinehart and Winston.

Kamil, M. (2004). *Adolescents and literacy: Reading for the 21st century.* Washington, DC: Alliance for Excellent Education.

Kane, S. (2003). *Literacy & learning in the content areas.* Scottsdale, AZ: Holcolm Hathaway.

Keen, E. O., & Zimmermann, S. (2007). *Mosaic of thought: The power of comprehension strategy instruction.* Portsmouth, NH: Heinemann.

Kornelly, D., & Smith, L. (1993). Bring back the USSR. *School Library Journal, 39*(4), 48.

Lent, R. (2006). *Engaging adolescent learners: A guide for content-area teachers.* Portsmouth, NH: Heinemann.

Lent, R. (2007). *Literacy learning communities: A guide for creating sustainable change in secondary schools.* Portsmouth, NH: Heinemann.

Leu, D. J., Leu, D. D., & Coiro, J. (2004). *Teaching with the Internet K–12: New literacies for new times* (4th ed.). Norwood, MA: Christopher-Gordon.

Levy, S. (2007, November 26). The future of reading. *Newsweek,* pp. 57–64.

Lewis, J., & Moorman, G. (2007). *Adolescent literacy instruction: Policies and promising practices.* Neward, DE: International Reading Association.

Marzano, R. J. (2004). *Building background knowledge for academic achievement: Research on what works in schools.* Alexandria, VA: Association for Supervision and Curriculum Development.

Marzano, R. J., Pickering, D., & Pollock, J. E. (2001). *Classroom instruction that works: Research-based strategies for increasing student achievement.* Washington, DC: Association for Supervision and Curriculum Development.

McKeown, M. G., Hamilton, R. L., Kucan, L., & Beck, I. L. (1997). *Questioning the author: An approach for enhancing student engagement with text.* Newark, DE: International Reading Association.

Moore, D. W., Bean, T. W., Birdyshaw, D., & Rycik, J. A. (1999). *Adolescent literacy: A position statement for the Commission on Adolescent Literacy of the International Reading Association.* Newark, DE: International Reading Association.

Nagy, W. E. (1988). *Teaching vocabulary to improve reading comprehension.* Newark, DE: International Reading Association.

National Center on Education and the Economy (NCEE). (2006). Tough choices for tough times: The report of the new commission on the skills of the American workforce—Executive Summary. In R. Heller & C. Greenleaf (Eds.), *Literacy instruction in the content areas: Getting to the core of middle and high school improvement* (p. 5). Washington, DC: Alliance for Excellent Education.

National Council of Teachers of English. (2004). *A call to action: What we know about adolescent literacy and ways to support teachers in meeting students' needs.* Retrieved May 26, 2008, from http://www.ncte.org/about/over/positions/category/read/118622.htm?source=gs

National Research Council. (2000). *How people learn: Brain, mind, experience, and school.* Washington, DC: National Academy Press.

Noddings, N. (2008, February). All our students thinking. *Educational Leadership, 65*(5), 8–13.

Osborn, P. (2001, Spring/Summer). Picture books for young adult readers. *The ALAN Review, 28*(3), 24.

Palincsar, A. S., & Brown, A. L. (1986). Interactive teaching to promote independent learning from text. *The Reading Teacher, 39*(8), 771–777.

Partnership for 21st Century Skills. (2007). U.S. students need 21st century skills to compete. Retrieved May 26, 2008, from http://www.21stcenturyskills.org/index2.php?option=com_content&task=view&id=369

Pearson, D. (2008, September). Teaching reading comprehension: Research, best practices and good teaching. Paper presented at the annual meeting of the Florida Reading Association, Orlando.

RAND Reading Study Group. (2003). *Reading for understanding: Toward an R & D program in reading comprehension.* Santa Monica, CA: Author.

Readence, J. E., Moore, D. W., Rickelman, R. J. (2000). *Pre-reading activities for content-area reading and learning* (3rd ed.). Newark, DE: International Reading Association.

Richison, J., Hernandez, A., & Carter, M. (2006). *Theme sets for secondary students: How to scaffold core literature.* Portsmouth, NH: Heinemann.

Ritchhart, R. (2004). *Intellectual character: What it is, why it matters, and how to get it.* San Francisco: Jossey-Bass.

Roberts, T., & Billings, L. (2008). Thinking is literacy, literacy thinking. *Educational Leadership, 65*(5), 32–36.

Sacks, P. (2001). *Standardized minds: The high price of America's testing culture and what we can do to change it.* Cambridge, MA: Da Capo Press.

Slavin, R. E., Cheung, A., Groff, C., & Lake, C. (2008, July/August/September). Effective reading programs for middle and high schools: A best-evidence synthesis. *Reading Research Quarterly, 443*(3), 290–322.

Smith, M. K. (2002, 2008). Howard Gardner and multiple intelligences. Retrieved July 16, 2008, from http://www.infed.org/thinkers/gardner.htm

Smith, M. W., & Wilhelm, J. D. (2002). *Reading don't fix no Chevys: Literacy in the lives of young men.* Portsmouth, NH: Heinemann.

Smith, M. W., & Wilhelm, J. (2006). *Going with the flow: How to engage boys (and girls) in their literacy learning.* Portsmouth, NH: Heinemann.

Taba, H. (1967). *Teacher's handbook for elementary social studies.* Reading, MA: Addison-Wesley.

Torgesen, J. (2007, June). Improving literacy in adolescents: The big ideas from research. PowerPoint presentation presented at the annual meeting of the Lexile National Reading Conference, Orlando.

Torgesen, J. K., Houston, D. D., Rissman, L. M., Decker, S. M., Roberts, G., Vaughn, S., Wexler, J., Francis, D. J., Rivera, M. O., & Lesaux, N. (2007). *Academic literacy instruction for adolescents: A guidance document from the Center on Instruction.* Portsmouth, NH: RMC Research Corporation, Center on Instruction.

Tovani, C. (2004). *Do I really have to teach reading?* Portland, ME: Stenhouse.

Valdes, G., Bunch, G., Snow, C., & Lee, C., with Matos, L. (2005). Enhancing the development of students' language(s). In L. Darling-Hammond & J. Bransford (Eds.), *Preparing teachers for a changing world: What teachers should learn and be able to do* (pp. 126–168). San Francisco: Jossey-Bass.

Warlick, D. (2004). *Redefining literacy for the 21st century.* Worthington, OH: Linworth.

Wiggins, G., & McTighe, J. (1998). *Understanding by design.* Alexandria, VA: Association for Supervision and Curriculum Development.

Wilhelm, J. (2007). *Engaging readers and writers with inquiry.* New York: Scholastic.

Wingert, P. (2008, May 19). Teens, tan and truth. *Newsweek.* Retrieved July 12, 2008, from http://www.newsweek.com/id/136310

Zarnowski, M. (2006). *Making sense of history: Using high-quality literature and hands-on experiences to build content knowledge.* New York: Scholastic.

Index

About the Author

ReLeah Cossett Lent, a secondary teacher for more than 20 years, spent several years at the University of Central Florida providing statewide literacy staff development. Now a national consultant, ReLeah facilitates the development of literacy leadership teams and professional learning communities within schools and districts, working closely with content-area teachers and their students. ReLeah is the author of several books and articles on literacy, including *Engaging Adolescent Learners* and *Literacy Learning Communities.* She and the co-author of her first two books, Gloria Pipkin, received the American Library Association's John Phillip Immroth Memorial Award and the NCTE/SLATE Intellectual Freedom Award. In addition, ReLeah won the 1999 PEN Newman's Own First Amendment Award.